The Economics of Vertical Disintegration

THE ECONOMICS
OF THE SERVICE SECTOR
IN CANADA

Series Editors:
Herbert G. Grubel
Michael A. Walker

The Economics of Vertical Disintegration

Donald G. McFetridge and Douglas A. Smith

THE FRASER INSTITUTE

This study is part of a general programme of research into the services sector made possible by a contribution from the Department of Regional Industrial Expansion, Government of Canada.

Canadian Cataloguing in Publication Data

McFetridge, D.G., 1945-

The economics of vertical disintegration

(The Economics of the service sector in Canada, ISSN 0835-4227)

Bibliography: p.

ISBN 0-88975-134-X

1. Service industries - Canada. 2. Contracting out - Canada. 3. Vertical integraion - Canada. I. Smith, Douglas A. II. Fraser Institute (Vancouver, B.C.). III. Title. IV. Series.

HD9985.C22M24 1988 338.4'7'000971 C88-091401-7

Printed in Singapore.

CONTENTS

TABLES

PREFACE AND SUMMARY

This study deals with the theory and measurement of contracting out. This subject is of significant importance for interpreting various empirical measures of service sector growth. In the extreme case, all service sector growth could be the result of the decisions of firms in other sectors to contract out services that previously were performed internally. The real economic significance of such shifts in the location of service production would be small. Our major objective has been to determine the proportion of service sector growth accounted for by contracting out. The theoretical framework that we develop in this study is based on transactions costs. In simplest terms, firms in the private sector determine the relative costs of internal and external production and choose the lower cost alternative. Relative production costs are of obvious importance and we assume that firms are always weighing these relative costs and making adjustments in the location of service production when profitable. However, our primary focus is on the transactions costs associated with the process of contracting out. These costs are associated with negotiating and enforcing the terms of contracts with external suppliers.

Changes in contracting out over time should be associated with changing relative costs of dealing with external suppliers. Contracting costs are lowered if a service becomes more standardized, that is, as its technical characteristics become better known and as the number of alternative suppliers increase. A change of this nature might be associated with growing demand implying a positive association between the service-intensity of an economy and the incidence of contracting out.

The three empirical measures of contracting out that we develop are based on data from the decennial census, the Census of Manufactures and the input-output table. These data are collected from households and establishments rather than from the firms on which our theoretical framework is based. This is a limitation of our study but in our opinion the empirical significance of this limitation is small.

Our first set of measures of contracting out is based on occupation by industry data from the census for 1961, 1971 and 1981. We infer contracting out of occupational employment by a specific industry if the share of industry employment accounted for by that occupation has decreased more or increased less than the proportion of total or economy-wide employment accounted for by the same occupation. For example, we infer that the manufacturing sector has contracted out janitorial employment if the ratio of janitors to all employees in manufacturing decreased more or increased less than the ratio of janitors to all employees measured on an economy-wide basis. We apply this method to four occupations: lawyers, accountants, security guards and janitors. For security guards, we find evidence of sustained and significant contracting out for both the 1961-1971 and 1971-1981 time periods. For accountants and janitors, we find substantial contracting out between 1971 and 1981 but none between 1961 and 1971. We can detect no contracting out of legal services in either time period.

Our second measure of contracting out uses data from the Census of Manufactures. It is defined as the ratio of non-production wages and salaries to value added less production wages and returns to capital. The substitution of purchased services for services previously produced internally should cause this ratio to decline. Using data for the time period 1961-1984, we find no evidence of the negative trend that would indicate contracting out.

The third set of measures is based on the input-output table. As an indicator of contracting out, we use the ratio of the value of purchased business services to industry wages, salaries and benefits. More external service purchases should cause this ratio to increase. We find that this ratio increased substantially over the 1961-1981 time period. We also find that the observed increase in this ratio is a consequence of the growth in the proportion of service inputs supplied by outside contractors rather than growth in the overall service intensity of production. Our only remaining reservation about these data has to do with the specific items included by Statistics Canada in the purchase of business services. Exploration of this point requires access to the large aggregation of the input-output table which we intend to pursue in future work.

Our study provides the basis for a thorough analysis of the determinants of contracting out. An area of potential interest in this regard is the role of labour unions. We argue that, subject to differences in transactions costs, unionized firms will have a greater incentive to contract out to lower cost external providers of services. In the study, we discuss the circumstances in which declining market power of trade unions will lead to more contracting out as opposed to concessions affecting the entire bargaining unit. We note, that although the union wage premium increases the incentive to contract out, union bargaining power can lead to contractual provisions limiting its extent. This makes inter-industry studies of the union impact on contracting out more difficult to interpret.

We conclude that there is sufficient indication of contracting out to warrant refinements and extensions of the measures developed in this study. For the 1971 to 1981 time period, our census-based measures indicate that for the four occupations considered, more than a quarter of service sector growth is the result of contracting out. Our input-output measures imply sustained and significant contracting out by virtually all sectors. These are important preliminary findings and suggest that a more complete understanding of contracting out is necessary if we are to interpret correctly the overall data on the growth of the service sector of the Canadian economy.

ABOUT THE AUTHORS

Donald G. McFetridge is a Professor of Economics at Carleton University in Ottawa. Dr. McFetridge received a B. Comm. in 1967 from the University of Saskatchewan and an M.A. in Economics from the University of Toronto in 1968. He attended the London School of Economics and received an M.Sc. in Economics in 1969 and then received a Ph.D. in Economics from the University of Toronto in 1971.

Dr. McFetridge has written and edited numerous books and articles on industrial organization and economic policy issues. He served as a Research Co-ordinator on the economics of industrial policy for the Royal Commission on the Economic Union and Development Prospects for Canada. His current research interests include the economics of competition policy and economic aspects of technology diffusion.

Douglas Smith is Associate Professor and Chairman in the Department of Economics at Carleton University. Dr. Smith received a B. Comm. in 1967 and an M.A. in Economics in 1968 from the University of Toronto and received a Ph.D. in Economics from the Massachusetts Institute of Technology in 1973. He joined Carleton University in 1972 and was a Visiting Associate Professor at the University of Virginia in 1978-79.

Dr. Smith's research interests are in the areas of labour economics, labour relations and the economics of property rights. His recent labour market research has focused on the causes and implications of the growing degree of divergence between the labour markets of Canada and the United States. His research on property rights deals primarily with copyright issues and on the policy aspects of the process of copyright revision.

Chapter I

INTRODUCTION

OVERVIEW

The rapid growth of the service sector of the Canadian economy has been widely documented. Many studies in this series of research projects investigate the experiences of particular service industries. This study is unique because it focuses on vertical disintegration or contracting out, a potentially important component of every service industry's growth. Vertical disintegration or contracting out refers to manufacturing and other firms' decisions to contract out services previously produced in-house to specialized suppliers in the service sector. The major hypothesis we will investigate is that since contracting out accounts for much of the service sector's growth, the existing data overstate the extent to which the Canadian economy is becoming more service-intensive.

Table 1
Share of Employment in the Service Sector
(Percentage of All Industries)

Year	Trade	Finance, Insurance and Real Estate	Services	Broad Service Sector
1961	15.3	3.5	19.5	38.3
1971	14.7	4.2	23.7	42.6
1981	16.9	5.4	29.3	51.6

Source: *Census of Canada*, 1961, 1971 and 1981.

SERVICE SECTOR GROWTH

The broadly defined service sector[1] has grown more rapidly than other sectors of the Canadian economy between 1961 and 1981. Table 1 shows that in 1961, this sector accounted for approximately 38 percent of total employment in Canada. By 1981, this had increased to nearly 52 percent of total employment. Empirically, it is clear that the service sector has become the largest single employer in the Canadian economy. Growth in service employment was greater between 1971 and 1981 than between 1961 and 1971, leading some analysts to predict a continuing high growth rate for this sector.

The policy implications of the service sector's growth are being considered in all of the studies in this series of research projects. Our study of service sector growth will examine how much growth results from contracting out or vertical disintegration. Consider a simple example. If a firm in the Canadian steel industry employs security guards and janitors, the data system counts these as manufacturing employees. However, these service inputs need not be produced internally. The firm can disintegrate vertically, that is, it can contract out these intermediate services to specialized service sector firms. In the case of these two occupations, we know that the corresponding service sector industries have grown substantially between 1961 and 1981. How much of this growth can be attributed to contracting out?

This question is important in order to interpret accurately the significance of service sector growth. In the example above, the real economic change involved is minimal. If contracting out has occurred, we presume that this reflects the greater efficiency of specialized production. But, the same services are being produced and the underlying service intensity of the Canadian economy is unchanged, despite an apparent decline in manufacturing intensity and an apparent increase in service intensity.

The analytical framework we use to assess this issue is based on transactions costs, an approach which recognizes the various ways production can be organized. Firms decide on the basis of cost minimization whether to produce service inputs internally or to purchase them with contracts from external suppliers. Of central importance in this decision is the cost of transacting with external suppliers. By using the transactions cost approach, we can identify the characteristics of exchanges that are less costly to produce within the firm and those that are less costly to contract from another firm.

Simple production cost differences are not sufficient to explain the pattern of contracting out. External suppliers can have a cost advantage in providing services, but services will continue to be provided internally if transactions costs exceed the production cost differential. Labour unions, for example, would generate an incentive to contract out if lower cost non-union suppliers are available, unless there are significant transactions costs. This issue is examined in a separate chapter of this study.

MEASUREMENT

We would like to establish the fraction of service sector growth that is attributable to contracting out. If this fraction is large, the policy issues associated with observed rates of service sector growth are less pressing. We have not found any studies which analyze the extent of vertical specialization in the detail necessary to answer the fundamental question of this study. Thus, our approach is exploratory and considers different measurement methods.

Our measures of service contracting out are based on three different data sources. Each will be analyzed in a separate chapter. The first set of data we will use consists of components of the occupation by industry matrices of the Census for the years 1961, 1971 and 1981. We will analyze data on four occupations from this source, each of which has a counterpart industrial classification in the service sector. These data and a number of assumptions about how requirements for these service inputs grow over time will be combined to produce estimates of contracting out. These estimates will be limited to four occupations.

One of the four occupations to be analyzed is the market for lawyers. We include this occupation because much of the analysis of service sector growth focuses on specialization in the production of professional services. Our estimates in this area will also be relevant to the theoretical literature on the organization of firms and the in-house monitoring of lawyers. Increased internal monitoring of lawyers implies a growth in corporate law departments and may imply a growth in contracting in rather than contracting out. Further insight will be provided by an analysis of contracting out in a very specialized sector of the legal market, namely specialists in patent and trademark law.

Next, we will use the annual Census of Manufactures to estimate changes over time in vertical specialization. The final source of data on contracting out we will use is the input-output table. Although we will use the medium aggregation, we acknowledge that confidential data contained in the large aggregation combined with data from the Census of Manufactures would provide even better contracting out estimates than the ones we develop.

UNIONS AND CONTRACTING OUT

In chapter six of this study, we will explore the relationship between unionization and contracting out in detail. We will argue that subject to the constraint of transactions costs, unionized firms will have an incentive to contract out to low-cost suppliers. Recently, competitive cost pressures for unionized firms have increased and have generated a number of collective cessions are likely to lead greater contracting out of work to specialized suppliers.

We will also examine contracting out or privatization of work usually performed by unionized public sector employees. Garbage collection is a prime example; it is frequently contracted out to the private sector. We will provide a survey of data which suggest private service production has increased in importance.

Contracting out is an important collective bargaining issue for unions. If unions are very strong, they could negotiate agreement provisions that would prevent contracting out by unionized employers. High union wages increase the employer's incentive to contract out, but union contract provisions may prevent such adjustments. We will analyze the extent of such barriers to contracting out in the manufacturing sector and in the portion of the public sector represented by the Canadian Union of Public Employees.

SCOPE AND LIMITATIONS

The analysis in this study is exploratory. We will provide a number of preliminary estimates of contracting out, but we recognize that each measure has a weakness. Our conclusions will suggest directions for further research and approaches for refining the preliminary calculations made in this study.

NOTE

1. Defined as Trade, Finance, Insurance and Real Estate and Services.

Chapter 2

THE THEORY OF VERTICAL INTEGRATION

DEFINING VERTICAL INTEGRATION

Vertical integration occurs when a single firm spans two or more stages of production. In Davies' (1987) words, backward integration occurs when a firm decides to *make* rather than *buy* an input from an independent supplier. Forward integration occurs when a firm decides to *use* rather than *sell* one of its products to independent customers.

Vertical transactions involve the sale of an intermediate good or service for use as an input in the production of another good or service. A vertical transaction is internal (an intra firm transaction) when the buying and selling companies are jointly owned. A vertical transaction is defined as a market or inter firm transaction when the buyer and seller have different owners.

These definitions do not tell how the endless variety of vertical relationships involving less than complete common ownership or long term or employment contracts should be classified. We draw on Williamson's (1979) analysis to distinguish three broad classes of vertical relationships:

> -Market Transactions: The relationship between the transacting parties has no value in itself. Unsatisfactory relationships are terminated.
>
> -Relational Transactions: The relationship between the transacting parties is valued for its own sake. Provisions are made for arbitrating disputes and ensuring performance.
>
> -Integration: The transacting parties are bound by common ownership (which pools the gains from trade) in a relationship which is not precisely defined and may change over time.

There have been some interesting attempts to explain the incidence and specific features of relational contracts.[1] The principal concern of this study is with the distinction between internal (intra firm) and all other forms of vertical exchange. Even within this narrow field, a number of unresolved definitional issues remain.

First, we must define the threshold of common ownership at which two corporate entities can be regarded as part of the same firm or, in Statistics Canada's terminology, enterprise. While minority ownership (with working control), majority ownership and full ownership do differ in regard to their respective incentive properties, these differences are too subtle (or our measurements too crude) to have been reflected in testable hypotheses.

Second, firms often rely on internal supplies for only a portion of a given input. Harrigan (1983) calls this taper integration. We must still decide what threshold proportion of internal supply a firm must reach to be regarded as being vertically integrated.[2]

Third, a number of common measures of vertical integration, including some used in this study, are not based on ownership. According to these measures, vertical integration occurs if successive stages of production are carried out within the same establishment. Vertical disintegration (or contracting out) occurs if successive stages of production are carried out in different establishments, regardless of whether they are commonly owned. Thus, although petroleum refining corporations may be relatively highly integrated vertically, establishment-based data may not reflect this fact. The same data may not show changes in the degree of vertical integration.

From an economic perspective, common ownership of production's successive stages is important. Enterprise-based measures of vertical integration are therefore preferable to the establishment-based measures with which we must often work.

Establishment and enterprise-based data on service inputs may not differ much, however. Ownership linkages between industrial firms and service sector firms such as law, accounting and janitorial service firms are uncommon. Contracting out these services almost certainly involves shifting to an independently-owned supplier.

Fourth, common ownership is not a helpful criterion for distinguishing employees of a firm from independent contractors. Cheung (1983) provides a good discussion of the problems involved in defining an employee. He begins with Coase's (1937) proposition that the firm's distinguishing characteristic is the replacement of the product market by the factor market. Rather than buy intermediate goods or services, an integrated firm hires the required factors of production and makes them. One could infer that salaried or hourly-rate workers should be defined as employees while piece-rate workers should be defined as independent suppliers.

The distinction is not this simple, however. Piece-rate contracts vary depending on whether the worker (i) works on-site; (ii) provides his own raw materials; (iii) provides his own tools; (iv) can employ others (subcontract); (v) sells to one customer at a time; (vi) sells to one customer over extended periods of time; (vii) accepts monitoring of his efforts.

Drawing on the insight of Acheson and McManus, Cheung argues that the means of payment chosen reflects whether effort or output is more readily measurable. He concludes that the means of payment alone does not define employee status. Furthermore, efforts to distinguish between employees and non-employees or between the firm and the market are futile.[3]

Grossman and Hart (1986) also argue that the form of remuneration is irrelevant to the distinction between employees and contractors. In their view, the distinction turns on the presence or absence of "residual control." Residual control exists when an agreement provides for contingent adaptation, the terms to be determined by one of the transacting parties. This is very similar to Coase's characterization of an intra-firm exchange as one involving a contract between a factor owner and an entrepreneur:

> ...whereby the factor for a certain remuneration (which may be fixed or fluctuating) agrees to obey the directions of the entrepreneur *within certain limits*. (1952, pp. 336-7)

Grossman and Hart use the example of insurance agents to illustrate the concept of residual (vertical) control. Insurance can be sold by employed agents, by independent, exclusive agents or by independent, non-exclusive agents (brokers). All are paid on commission. Employers and exclusive agents cannot take their clients to other insurance companies. By retaining control over the list of clients, an insurance company exercises residual control. Brokers are free to take their clients elsewhere; in this sense, they exercise residual control. Both employed and independent but exclusive agents should be defined as employees, while brokers should be viewed as independent contractors.

Grossman and Hart's reasoning implies that as far as economic incentives and behaviour are concerned, independent but exclusive retail or wholesale distributors are the same as manufacturer-owned dealerships. Similarly, the distinguishing characteristic of an employee may be that he lacks the right to work for others (during the contract period) or to subcontract assigned tasks. An employee does not have residual control while an independent contractor does.

ALTERNATIVE EXPLANATIONS OF VERTICAL INTEGRATION

There are a number of recent survey articles, including Perry (1987) and Davies (1987), which provide taxonomies of the motives for vertical integration. All agree that there are three "fundamental" motives for vertical integration: (i) technological interdependence (economies of vertical scope), (ii) transactions costs and (iii) imperfect competition. Williamson's (1975, 1986) argument is widely accepted: Technological interdependence is important only insofar as it affects transactions costs. This leaves two alternative approaches to vertical integration theory: the transactions cost approach and the imperfect competition approach.

According to the transactions cost approach, the number of potential transactions between stages of production is virtually limitless. The interesting question is how these transactions are organized. Vertical integration is a way of organizing a vertical transaction when intra-firm exchange is less costly than inter-firm (market) exchange. The essence of the transactions cost approach lies in the identification of the characteristics of transactions which makes them less costly to conduct within a firm. More generally, Williamson (1979) argues that the transactions cost approach can be used to explain observed differences in the organization of inter-firm transactions as well as the incidence of vertical integration.

The imperfect competition approach also recognizes the central role of transactions costs. According to the imperfect competition approach, exchange will always be organized in a way that minimizes the transactions costs. Observed contractual forms or governance structures are always cost-minimizing, so explaining their incidence is both methodologically difficult and uninteresting.[4] The adherents of the imperfect competition approach are more interested in identifying potential vertical transactions than in the way these transactions are organized.

Perry (1987) is an exponent of the imperfect competition approach, which he calls the imperfect markets approach. He says that imperfect competition or uncertainty or information asymmetries may lead to additional gains from trade between stages of production. These gains are then exploited in the organizationally most efficient manner by the parties involved.

The imperfect competition approach will be familiar to readers of undergraduate textbooks in industrial organization. Successive monopolies, bilateral monopolies and upstream monopolies with variable input proportions downstream can all yield price-output outcomes that can be improved upon either by vertical integration or by contractual arrangements between stages of production (Waterson, 1984, Ch. 5).

More recent developments in the imperfect competition approach include the investigation of the circumstances leading to so-called vertical restrictions, including resale price maintenance, exclusive dealing and exclusive territories (Mathewson and Winter, 1985). Monopolistic competition among retailers and imperfectly informed retail buyers can cause retail prices and promotional effort that are inappropriate from the manufacturer's point of view. Mutually beneficial changes in prices and promotion can be effected either by contractual vertical restrictions or by vertical integration.

This literature illustrates how the imperfect competition and transactions cost approaches complement each other. The imperfect competition literature identifies the margins on which observed vertical restrictions are intended to operate. The transactions cost approach explains the institutions in which they are embedded.

We are more concerned with explaining and measuring the extent of changes in the institutions involved in a broad range of vertical transactions than with explaining why particular vertical transactions occur. Thus, we rely on the transactions cost approach, the focus of the next three sections of this chapter. We use the imperfect competition approach when we analyze the effect of unionization on the incentive to specialize vertically in chapter 6.

THE ELEMENTS OF THE TRANSACTIONS COST APPROACH

The transactions cost approach is based on the following assumptions:

1. The unit of analysis is the transaction.
2. There are a variety of institutional arrangements called governance structures within which a transaction can be conducted.
3. Governance structures vary fundamentally in the behavioral incentives they imply for the transacting parties.
4. Choosing a governance structure essentially involves choosing the incentives which maximize the gains from trade.
5. The incentive system which maximizes the gains from trade depends on the characteristics of the transaction.
6. There is a continuum of governance structures ranging from what we call classical contracting to unified governance. A transaction carried out under unified governance is also called an intra-firm or internal transaction.
7. The transactions cost approach to vertical integration predicts the characteristics of vertical transactions carried out under unified governance.

CHARACTERISTICS OF INTERNAL VERTICAL TRANSACTIONS

According to the transactions cost hypothesis, one or both parties must make irreversible specialized investments in internal transactions. According to Williamson:

> The main factor that is responsible for vertical integration from a transaction-cost point of view is asset specificity. Take this away and autonomous contracting between successive production stages has good economizing properties in respect of both production cost and transactions cost. As asset specificity increases, however, the balance shifts in favour of internal organization. (1986, p. 157)

Asset specificity leads to integration for two reasons. First, the existence of transaction-specific assets causes the parties to become locked into their relationship. It is costly to turn to alternative buyers (sellers). The result is *ex post* bilateral monopoly with the attendant incentive for opportunistic attempts to redistribute the gains from trade. Vertical integration attenuates the incentive for redistributive activity. The buyer and seller are commonly owned. Their profit streams are pooled. Little or nothing can be gained by either party from increasing one profit stream at the expense of the other. McKean (1971) argues thus:

> Because of this altered claim structure, it is now less rewarding to management of the components division to haggle with management of the processing division (and *vice versa*). It is less rewarding than before to exchange dubious information or engage in strategic bargaining. It becomes more rewarding than before for personnel in all divisions to accept monitoring by overall management. Employees find that fiats by the new management are less costly and/or more rewarding to them than when their rights were linked to the profits of different firms. Now that they are rewarded for veracity to the new management and contributions to overall profits, the divisions can trust each other and work harmoniously to a greater extent. Informal tacitly understood contracts become enforceable and are efficient more often than before. (p. 124)

Second, the requirement for specialized investment implies that the transaction involved has at least an element of uniqueness to it. It is, in Williamson's terms, "idiosyncratic." In the limiting case there are either no other buyers or no other sellers *ex post*. Thus, the magnitude of the scale economies foregone by confining production to internal needs is likely to be small. In contrast, if the transaction is not unique (transaction- specific assets are unimportant), there will be a number of alternative users (or suppliers) *ex post*. The scale economies foregone by confining production to internal needs may be considerable. This will occur if optimal scales at successive stages of production are incompatible.

The internalization of a transaction saves resources which would have been devoted to redistributing the gains from trade; but it may also involve sacrificing economies of scale in production. The greater the importance of transaction-specific assets the more likely it is that the former exceeds the latter. In Williamson's (1979) terms:

> For some transactions a shift from one [governance] structure to another may permit a simultaneous reduction in both the expense of writing a complex contract (which economizes on bounded rationality) and the expense of executing it effectively in an adaptive sequential way (by attenuating opportunism). Indeed this is precisely the attraction of internal procurement for transactions of a recurrent, idiosyncratic kind. Not only are market aggregation economies negligible for such transactions - since the requisite investments are transaction specific - but market trading in these assets is shot through with appropriable quasi-rent hazards. (p. 246)

Transaction specificity can take a number of forms. These include, first, site specificity. In this case successive stages of production are located in close proximity and relocation costs are significant. Site specificity is often associated with technological interdependence between successive stages of production. Klein et al. (1978) cited body stamping and automobile assembly as an example of two stages of production which have historically been located in close geographic proximity.

Second, while they may be mobile geographically, the physical characteristics of assets may be transaction-specific. In the extreme, tools or components may be specialized to one user or supplier. It is more likely that alternative users or suppliers exist, but it is too costly to turn to them in the middle of a transaction. Monteverde and Teece (1982) and Masten (1984) have investigated how widespread component specificity in automobile and aerospace production is. Palay (1984) documented differences in user specificity of various types of railway freight cars.

Human capital may also be specialized to one user. This is especially likely if non-transferable learning occurs during the course of a transaction. In this case an employee or a supplier acquires experience which gives him an advantage over potential competitors. His experience is less (or even not) valuable to alternative employers or customers, however. Consequently, it is costly for both employer and employee (supplier and customer) to go elsewhere. Each will take advantage of this situation and attempt to appropriate a greater share of the experience-related productivity benefit. Williamson, Wachter and Harris (1975) argued that the solution to this problem lies in the so-called internal labour market which makes use of job-specific rather than employee-specific experience ratings.

In the context of vertical integration, Monteverde and Teece (1982) argued that non-transferable learning is a feature of the supply of new, engineering-intensive automobile components. More generally, it could be argued that non-transferable learning occurs when new tasks are performed or new inputs supplied. The importance of this learning would decline as the task or input involved became more widely practised or used. In this case, a negative relationship between the novelty of a task or input and the incidence of contracting-out would exist. Evidence cited by Stigler (1951) and Silver (1984) that "new" industries tend to be more vertically integrated is consistent with this proposition.

As currently interpreted, the transactions cost hypothesis attributes vertical integration principally to asset specificity. This interpretation is popular with applied economists: Asset specificity is potentially measurable so that its hypothetical relationship with the incidence of internal exchange is testable. Some of these tests will be discussed in the next section.

Although it has facilitated empirical work, the current interpretation of the hypothesis is at least potentially misleading. First, as Williamson has pointed out, the degree of asset specificity is not given exogenously. It is chosen by the transacting parties in order to maximize the gains from trade.

The optimal degree of transaction-specific investment depends, in turn, on the extent to which optimal scales at successive stages of production coincide. If, for example, optimal scale at stage one is five times optimal scale at stage two, it will be costly in terms of scale economies foregone to dedicate stage one facilities to a single stage two user. Stage one location and product characteristics will be chosen so as to allow for multiple users. When optimal scales differ markedly from stage to stage, we should observe neither specialized investments for a single buyer or seller nor internal transactions. The more compatible the optimal scales and scopes of successive stages of production are, the smaller the production cost disadvantage of specializing assets for a single buyer or seller will be and the more likely specialized assets (hence potential hold-up problems) and internalization will be observed.

Recognition of the fundamental role of scale and scope compatibility in the vertical integration decision provides a link between the transactions cost approach and both the management strategy literature and the earlier theories of vertical integration. The literature on managerial strategy cites "unbalanced throughput" (scale and scope incompatibility) as the principal limitation on vertical integration (Buzzell, 1983; Harrigan, 1983; Marriotti and Caincara, 1986; Casson, 1987).

Stigler's (1951) theory of vertical integration and disintegration is based, at least in part, on scale incompatibility. The Stigler hypothesis is that vertical disintegration is a consequence of market growth (and vertical integration is a consequence of market decline). Stigler argues that the growth of downstream demand (and thus the derived demand for intermediate inputs) facilitates specialization in the supply of these inputs. If the scale of downstream firms remains the same, however, the gains from upstream specialization can only be realized if each upstream specialist supplies an increasing number of downstream users.

In essence, the Stigler hypothesis is that the growth of the downstream market increases the degree of scale incompatibility between the first and second stages of production resulting in vertical disintegration. If the growth of downstream demand also resulted in an increase in the scale of downstream production, the degree of scale incompatibility need not increase. It may even decrease. In this case downstream market growth would cause vertical integration rather than disintegration.

There are ways to solve a scale or scope incompatibility problem while maintaining common ownership of successive stages of production. One solution is "taper integration." Each stage of production exploits all potential scale and scope economies selling output in excess of internal requirements (buying intermediate inputs in excess of internal production) to (from) independent firms.

It would appear that, given the option of taper integration, there is nothing to deter common ownership of successive stages of production even where internal vertical transactions constitute a small fraction of total activity. This is where the other incentive effects of internalization come into play.

As we argued above, common ownership of successive stages of production has the benefit of reducing the incidence of opportunistic hold-ups on transactions between them. The fewer or smaller the transactions, the smaller are the potential savings.

Common ownership also changes the general incentives of divisions operating at each stage of production. Divisional profits are an arbitrary component of the pooled income stream. Divisional shortcomings are less readily detectable and their consequences are borne in part by other divisions. Additional resources must be devoted to monitoring divisional performance. The loss in profit due to the deterioration of divisional performance (shirking) plus the cost of additional monitoring must be compared with the reduction in the cost of interdivisional transactions. The smaller or less frequent interdivisional transactions are, the less likely it is that common ownership will yield a net gain.

McManus (1975) made this point and noted that, disregarding tax considerations, the integration of two firms between whom there are no potential transactions is unambiguously wealth-reducing. The implication of this argument is that a limit exists on the extent to which taper integration can solve the problem of scale or scope incompatibility. At some point intra-firm vertical transactions become relatively unimportant; their incentive advantages are overwhelmed by the overall incentive disadvantage of the integrated vertical structure.

Williamson's earlier work argued that the likelihood of internalization increases with the incidence of small numbers, uncertainty and information asymmetries. Klein et al. (1978) reduced this list to one factor, (*ex post*) small numbers resulting from specialized investments. They reasoned that it is costly to remedy hold-ups even when they are obvious, that is, even when obligations are clearly specified and all the relevant circumstances are known (1978). This is an empirical question. It appears undisputable, however, that the scope for opportunistic behaviour is greater when obligations have not been fully specified *ex ante* (due to uncertainty) and all the circumstances relevant to the determination of performance obligations are not known to both parties (information asymmetry).

Not only do uncertainty and information asymmetries remain important if not necessary conditions for internalization to be advantageous, they also help to explain variations in the forms of vertical integration observed. For example, Globerman and Schwindt (1986) observed that pulp mills integrate backwards into logging for part of their requirements as a means of monitoring their independent suppliers' performance. Worthy (1984) noted that the policy of Sears Roebuck was to be the most important but not the only customer of its (independent) suppliers. The latter were obliged "to fight for enough non-Sears business to realize a satisfactory overall corporate profit." In addition to providing Sears with an indication of their suppliers' competitiveness, this practice also provided the suppliers with an indicator of both Sears' competitiveness and the state of the product market. Uncertainty may also be responsible in part for the observation by Stigler (1951) and Silver (1984) that "new" industries tend to source more of their inputs internally than "mature" industries.

In conclusion, although asset specificity is a necessary condition for internalization, it is not sufficient and should not, in any case, be treated as an exogenous variable in empirical work. Equally relevant to a transactions cost explanation of vertical integration are the following:

- scale and scope compatibility
- information asymmetries

- uncertainty
- potential transaction size and frequency.

TESTS OF THE TRANSACTIONS COST HYPOTHESIS

Cross-sectional statistical tests of the transactions cost hypothesis have been conducted by Monteverde and Teece (1982), Masten (1984), Levy (1985) and Anderson and Schmittlein (1984). Monteverde and Teece investigated the determinants of the probability of General Motors and Ford producing individual automobile components in-house. They found that the probability a component is produced in- house increases with the engineering effort required to design it and is greater for components specific to one assembler. They took both variables as indicators of potential hold-up problems due to human and physical capital specificity and interpreted their results as supporting evidence for the transactions cost hypothesis.

Masten attempted to distinguish between the characteristics of components rated as *make* or *buy* by a panel of aerospace procurement managers. He found that make components tend to be more complex and more specialized than buy components. Components which are both specialized and complex had the highest probability of being rated make components. He also found that neither the locational specificity nor the distinction between standard and moderately complex components mattered.

Levy investigated the determinants of interfirm differences in vertical integration as measured by the value added to shipments ratio. He found no relationship between vertical integration and his measure of site-specificity, the average distance products are shipped. It is not clear whether his distance measure covers intermediate products (as it should) or final products.

Levy found a positive relationship between vertical integration and either plant or firm concentration. He argued that the concentration variables are proxies for the incidence of transaction-specific capital. A more defensible interpretation is that inter-industry differences in the ratio of quasi-rent (and possibly monopoly rent) to shipments, and hence the ratio of value added to shipments, are a function of industry concentration. There is a similar explanation for Levy's finding of a (weak) positive relationship between R&D intensity and vertical integration. R&D expenditures are included in value added.

Levy also found a negative relationship between vertical integration and the rate of growth of shipments holding lagged vertical integration constant. He interpreted this as support of the Stigler hypothesis.

Anderson and Schmittlein analyzed the factors which determine the use of company sales personnel as opposed to independent distributors in the marketing of various electronic components. Company sales staff tend to be used when (i) special training is required to sell the product, (ii) detailed knowledge of clients is required, (iii) detailed and/or proprietary knowledge of the selling company is required, (iv) a continuing relationship between sales people and clients is required and (v) "output" measures of performance of sales personnel are unreliable. These results are consistent with transactions cost reasoning.

Recent case studies of vertical integration which adopt a transactions cost framework include Eccles (1981), Casson (1987), Globerman and Schwindt (1986) and Mariotti and Caincara (1986).

The characteristics of vertical integration in the construction industry were studied by Eccles and by Casson. Eccles investigated subcontracting in various trades by a sample of small general contractors in Massachusetts. He found that most trades are subcontracted. He attributed this to the relatively short duration of most jobs and the absence of job-specific investment. The implied ability to sever the relationship disciplined both parties.

The incidence of subcontracting is greater in the specialized trades (electricians, plumbers, drywallers) than in carpentry and the unskilled trades. This is, at least in part, a consequence of scale incompatibility. These small contractors could not keep specialists occupied full time at their trade, but carpenters and unskilled workers could fill their time with various tasks as required.

Casson argued that concern over quality control in crucial areas such as electrical work limits subcontracting. This proposition is not supported by Eccles's findings. Also Casson made the questionable assumption that the quality of electrical work is less readily discerned on inspection than the quality of other trades' work. Casson also found that the largest general contractors in Britain are not integrated vertically to any extent. Existing backward integration is into pre-cast concrete and aggregates (stone, gravel). The reason for this may be the site-specificity of suppliers of these inputs.

Globerman and Schwindt (1986) investigated the nature and incidence of vertical integration in the Canadian forest products industry and attempted to explain it in transactions cost terms. They found that the largest newspapers tend to be integrated backward into newsprint production. Newsprint manufacturers are all integrated backward into pulp production. There is some backward integration into logging and little or none into transportation. They attributed the integration of pulp and paper production to site-specificity. Once installed, newsprint machines are effectively specialized to a few customers, thereby creating potential hold-up problems which can be reduced by vertical integration.[5]

The authors puzzled over the direction of internal control in vertical newspaper-newsprint combinations. Why is the newsprint mill a subsidiary of the newspaper rather than *vice versa*? From the standpoint of reducing transactions costs, all that matters is that the two operations are jointly owned. The lines of internal control will presumably radiate from the division(s) best placed to co-ordinate the assembly and disposition of the final product.[6]

Casson (1987) discussed the possible motives for backward integration by shippers into ocean shipping and measured horizontal and vertical integration by British shipping companies. Some of the motives for integration he presented are consistent with transactions cost reasoning. For example, backward integration is more likely when (i) the shipper's throughput is sufficient to fully utilize a discrete number of vessels of efficient size (scale compatibility), (ii) the shipper is sending goods to or from an isolated port where alternative cargoes and vessels are scarce (site specificity) and (iii) the shipper is burdened with high capacity (fixed) costs, or the product shipped is perishable. The last two sets of circumstances entail greater potential hold-up problems which can be reduced by integration.

Casson found no link between the nature of the vessel and the incidence of vertical integration. He explained that although ships may be specialized in use, they are unlikely to be specialized to a user on a worldwide basis. Thus, ships differ from railway cars.[7] Early in their development, however, shipper ownership of oil tankers and refrigerated cargo ships was more common than it is today. This fact is consistent with Stigler's (1951) and Silver's (1984) observation that new inputs and new industries are more likely to be sourced or to source internally.

Mariotti and Caincara (1986) measured and explained changes in vertical integration in the Italian textile-clothing industry. They found that between 1971 and 1981 firms tended to become horizontally more diversified and vertically more specialized. Moreover, the extent of horizontal diversification fluctuated with fashion trends.

The authors argued that know-how is stage-specific but transferable across product lines. Consequently, opportunities for diversification differ from stage-to-stage. Full vertical integration prevents each stage from fully exploiting its know-how. This is a good example of scope (as opposed to scale) incompatibility. Apparently, the degree of scope incompatibility has become greater since 1971.

Chandler (1961) anticipated much of the transactions cost reasoning presented above. She examined the impact of jet engines' introduction on the maintenance activities of U.S. airlines. The airlines had maintained their own piston engines. Jet engine maintenance required new skills and facilities, but jet engines needed to be serviced less frequently. Maintenance practices and routines probably became more similar across airlines and engine types. The result was, first, a divergence in optimal scales (individual airline maintenance needs fell relative to the optimal scale of maintenance activity) and, second, standardization of maintenance procedures. Independent engine maintenance specialists eventually replaced internal service departments.

Transactions costs have also been adduced as explanations of the incidence of both long-term contracts and multinational enterprises. With respect to contractual relationships, Palay (1984) found that the relationship between railways and shippers differed markedly depending on whether the freight cars involved are specialized to the user. Relationships involving unspecialized cars are disciplined principally by the threat of severance and are generally less likely to provide for adjustment to new circumstances. Relationships involving specialized cars are governed by "mutuality of interest" (both parties have quasi-rents at stake) and contain provisions for short-term and long-term adjustment. Palay also observed several examples of vertical integration in which shippers own highly specialized cars.

Joskow (1987) analyzed the duration of contracts between coal mines and electrical utilities. He found that duration is longer when the utility is located at the mine site (site-specific investment). Duration is also an increasing function of the quantity of coal contracted for. Duration does not appear to depend on the extent of user specialization to a particular type of coal.

Recent surveys of the relevant literature on multinationals have been written by Teece (1986) and Casson (1987, 1987a). Caves (1982) summarized the earlier literature. The consensus of this literature is that multinationals tend to be prominent in industries in which firm-specific intangible assets such as brand recognition, know-how and technology are important. Meredith (1984) confirmed this is true for Canada. The implication of these findings is that arm's length transfers of intangibles must be relatively costly.

Davidson and McFetridge (1984, 1985) and McFetridge (1986) argued that transactions cost reasoning implies that the relative cost of internal transactions depends on the characteristics of the intangible assets involved. Furthermore, initial transfers of new and radical technologies are more likely to be internal; research confirmed this proposition.

IS THE TRANSACTIONS COST HYPOTHESIS TAUTOLOGICAL?

The empirical work surveyed in the previous section has some potentially serious methodological defects. First, some of the explanatory variables employed are not exogenous, particularly the measures of asset specificity. The degree of asset specificity is jointly determined with the mode of transacting. The appropriate empirical approach is to specify and estimate asset specificity and transaction mode equations simultaneously. This requires, in turn, much better measures of some of the underlying determinants of the cost of internalization (scale compatibility, scope compatibility, novelty of products or processes involved) than are currently available.

Second, researchers did not test the hypothesis that transactions costs are minimized; they assumed it. They tested the hypothesis that asset specificity increases the relative cost of market transactions. They also test the hypothesis that transportation cost, for example, is a good indicator of or proxy for asset specificity. Failure to reject the null may imply any or all of the following:

- The proxy is not a good indicator of asset specificity.
- The relative cost of market transactions does not increase with asset specificity.
- The parties do not minimize transactions costs.

Similarly, the null may be rejected for the wrong reason such as in Levy's (1984) work when the measures of asset specificity are definitionally related to the measure of vertical integration.

One way to overcome this problem is to model more explicitly the circumstances leading to internalization. There have been a number of recent attempts, including Ethier (1986), Grossman and Hart (1986) and Horstman and Markusen (1986, 1987), to move in this direction.

Ethier examined a situation in which an upstream manufacturer performed cost-reducing R&D on behalf of a downstream distributor. The outcome of the manufacturer's R&D effort depended, in part, on the influence of random factors. The downstream distributor could neither observe the quality of the upstream R&D effort directly nor infer it from its outcome. A poor outcome can always be attributed by the manufacturer to the influence of random factors (the state of nature) rather than to poor effort. While the distributor could elicit the appropriate R&D effort from the manufacturer by making his payments contingent on the amount of cost reduction achieved (an incentive compatible contract), Ethier assumed that a contract of this nature is too costly to write and vertical integration is the only option. In this way, Ethier linked information asymmetries, uncertainty and vertical integration to each other.

Grossman and Hart analyzed the circumstances under which one firm will purchase the residual right of control in another. Ownership of the residual right of control does not necessarily imply residual claimant status (equity ownership); nor does it imply full vertical (or horizontal) integration in which joint profits are maximized. It implies only the right to make *ex post* output or quality decisions for which, by assumption, *ex ante* contracts can not be written.

Their analysis leads to the intuitively plausible prediction that there will be no transfer of the residual right of control (non-integration) if the respective profits of each firm are not sensitive to the *ex ante* non-contractible decisions of the other. Residual control of firm j by firm i is (second best) optimal if the profits of j are not sensitive to the non-contractible decisions of either firm.

Grossman and Hart applied their model to the explanation of vertical integration in insurance marketing. They distinguished between employed or exclusive agents who can not take clients to other insurers (and thus do not have the residual right of control) and insurance brokers who can take clients elsewhere (and thus do have the residual right of control). They predicted that brokers would be more important in the marketing of property, casualty and automobile insurance for which renewal is relatively sensitive to (non-contractible) agent effort than in the marketing of life insurance in which renewal is not sensitive to agent effort. Their research validated this prediction.

According to Horstman and Markusen (1987), internalization occurs because it is impossible by assumption to write a contract which would induce a licensee to provide the quality of product which the licensor wishes to provide. If quality is ascertainable by inspection (rather than after purchase) or if the licensee can be made to bear the entire cost of the diminution of the licensor's reputation resulting from cheating on quality (say by reciprocal licensing), then licensing dominates.

These three papers improved on the traditional transactions cost methodology in that internalization is the result of a formal optimization process. They all assumed, however, that some contracts can not be written and did not state why some contracts can not be written. (Williamson began his research with these problems.) Moreover, the qualitative predictions of all three of these models are the same as if they were derived from the admittedly less rigorous traditional transactions cost approach. Internalization is more likely to occur when (a) the degree of technological uncertainty is high (Ethier), (b) the effect of either party's non-verifiable efforts on the profits of the other is high (Grossman and Hart) and (c) both the information asymmetry regarding product quality and the sunk investment in reputation is high (Horstman and Markusen).

IMPLICATIONS FOR CONTRACTING OUT TO THE SERVICE SECTOR

The ultimate goal of this study is to measure the extent of contracting out to the service sector and to determine the causes of it. In this section, we will discuss the role transactions cost theory of vertical integration plays in furthering our understanding of the contracting out (disintegration) of service functions.

According to transactions cost theory, services formerly performed internally will tend to be contracted out under two sets of circumstances: (l) if the scale at which the service can be produced efficiently increases relative to the amount used by individual customers and (2) if the service involved becomes more standardized, that is, less customer-specific and more widely used.

Operationalization of the theory requires the measurement of changes in scale disparity, standardization and their respective sources. With respect to scale incompatibility, there are two possibilities. The first is the Stigler (1951) hypothesis that it is associated with the growth of the using industries. In the simplest terms, other things being equal, the rate of contracting out should be greater in the industries which are growing faster. As the discussion above concludes, however, industry growth and vertical disintegration are associated only if successive stages of production differ with respect to potential scale economies (ie., the scale elasticity of unit cost varies from stage to stage).

Scale disparities can also be aggravated by growth in the supplying industries themselves. This would occur if new uses are found for intermediate inputs. This may have occurred in the legal services industry. Growth in the demand for legal services has resulted in the specialization in various forms of litigation as well as securities, labour, real estate and intellectual property law.

The more specialized the lawyer, the less likely it is that a single client can fully utilize his skills. Thus, these legal specialists should be found in law firms while corporate law departments perform functions which either are less specialized in terms of legal knowledge or are highly client-specific. Carr and Mathewson (1987) have argued that corporate law departments will, in addition, perform the function of monitoring outside counsel.

The empirical implications of this argument are, first, that relative spending on outside counsel either across firms or over time depends on the demand of the firms involved for specialized legal knowledge. Second, given the needs of the firms involved and the degree of specialization by lawyers, relative spending on in-house counsel by industrial firms should increase with firm size. Carr and Mathewson provided some rough cross section evidence in support of the second proposition. This issue is discussed in more detail in Chapter 3.

A second general source of increased scale disparities is technological change. A good example is the case of aircraft engine maintenance discussed earlier. The switch from piston to jet engines involved a fixed cost: the acquisition of new maintenance skills and equipment. Since jet engines need servicing less frequently than piston engines, the maintenance requirements of individual airlines declined. Full utilization of the fixed investment in skills and facilities required that maintenance specialists serve several airlines.

Transactions involving intermediate inputs—including service inputs—are likely to become more standardized as the production technology of the input in question matures. If the using industry is also new this should coincide with its maturation. As noted previously, both Stigler (1951) and Silver (1984) cited historical evidence supporting the relationship between input (and using industry) maturity and vertical disintegration. Casson's (1987) observation that petroleum tankers and refrigerated cargo ships tended to be shipper-owned early in their development also supports this line of reasoning.

While the concept of input or industry maturity may be useful in an historical context, it would appear to have limited predictive value. It is usually possible to define maturity only retrospectively. It may be possible to use direct and indirect R&D intensity as an indicator of maturity at the industry level. Similarly, the number of years in use might serve to indicate maturity at the individual input level. Again, empirical work tells us as much about the quality of these proxies as it does about the relationship between maturity, standardization and the cost of transacting.

A service input category to which the maturity hypothesis might apply is computer systems analysis and programming. For practical purposes, this occupation did not exist in the industrial sector prior to 1960. The maturity hypothesis would predict an increasing tendency for industrial sector firms to contract out programming and systems analysis (holding scale compatibility constant) in recent years. An analysis of U.S. data over the period 1970-80, while extremely crude, does not appear to support this prediction (McCracken, 1985, pp. 20-1).

The details of our analysis of the role of unionization in the explanation of contracting out appear in chapter 6. We will confine ourselves to a discussion of the links between the transactions cost and unionization explanations of contracting out. Much of the earlier concern of unions over contracting out (prior to 1970) was over loss of membership to other unions rather than to non-union employment. During this period, contracting out may have occurred for the transactions cost reasons given above with relative wage considerations being less important.

More recently, contracting out has tended to involve the replacement of unionized with non-unionized sources of supply. Increased off-shore competition has played a crucial role here. The ability to move one or more stages of production offshore has effectively given domestic industrial employers a non-union alternative at these stages of production. Confronted with this alternative, domestic unions have acquiesced in the use of local non-union suppliers.

The unionization explanation of contracting out is, in essence, that it is a consequence of the erosion of the monopoly power of domestic trade unions. This decline in union power is the result of increased foreign competition in both final and intermediate products. This phenomenon should be especially apparent in industries characterized by physically separable stages of production, readily transferable technologies, widely available labour skills and low transportation costs and other barriers to trade.[8]

The nature of the concessions made by individual unions (including the extent to which this involves contracting out) will be discussed in chapter 6. Transactions cost considerations continue to be relevant because they help to determine the net advantage to employers of using independent non-union sources of supply.

NOTES

1. See Joskow (1987) and references therein.
2. Monteverde and Teece (1982) test hypotheses about the determinants of vertical integration employing alternative thresholds. This is potentially troublesome in that the definition and the hypotheses are being tested simultaneously. In this case the authors' inferences are not sensitive to small changes in the definition of vertical integration.
3. Eccles (1981, p. 352) finds that in the construction industry almost half of all subcontracting involves labour only (employer provides materials and tools). He concludes:

   In many cases the distinction between employees and subcontractors can be a very fuzzy one indeed. This is especially true given the fact that the builders indicated that some of their subcontractors worked almost exclusively for them.
4. According to this view empirical tests of the transactions cost hypothesis are really testing alternative measures of the cost of transacting not cost-minimizing behaviour.
5. The location of the mill and the newspaper should also matter here as should the scale of the newspaper operation.
6. Grossman and Hart (1986) suggest additional factors bearing upon the direction of vertical control.
7. See the discussion of Palay (1984) in this section.
8. For an elaboration see Grunwald and Flamm (1985).

Chapter 3

MEASURING CONTRACTING OUT USING THE DECENNIAL CENSUS

APPROACH

In this chapter, we will analyze contracting out in the case of four narrowly defined occupational groups in the published Standard Occupational Classification (SOC). These four occupations have corresponding industry classifications in the Standard Industrial Classification (SIC). These four groups are the following:

- Accountants (SOC-1171); accounting services (SIC-861).
- Security guards (SOC-6115); security services (SIC-855).
- Janitors (SOC-6191); services to buildings (SIC-898).
- Lawyers (SOC-2343); legal services (SIC-866).

The basis for our analysis is the occupation by industry data of the Census of Canada in 1961, 1971 and 1981. These data are not fully comparable across census years. However, for the occupations we analyze the impact of changing labour force and occupational definitions is small. Statistics Canada provided the 1981 data according to both the 1971 and 1981 definitions for the four-digit SOC categories we use. A comparison of the 1981 data compiled according to 1971 definitions and according to 1981 definitions shows only small differences. The largest discrepancy is for janitors (SOC-6191). The occupational totals for this group are 1.8 percent smaller using 1981 definitions. Given the inherent imprecision in our estimating procedures, we conclude that data problems are unlikely to bias our results.

An example illustrates our approach in using these data. For a particular occupation, one can tabulate actual employment levels in each of the three years. The employment of security guards, for example, is spread across all industries. We use 1961 as a base year and consider two scenarios to "predict" employment levels by industry for security guards in 1971 and 1981. We assume first that in every industry, the number of security guards per unit of output grows at the economy-wide rate. The second assumption is that the number of security guards per employee grows at the economy-wide rate. The extent of contracting out is determined by comparing actual employment levels in 1971 and 1981 with these two predicted levels.

This method can be demonstrated most clearly by focusing on a single occupation. For all accountants, the actual number of accountants in 1971 (A_{71}) can be expressed as follows:

$$A_{71} = E_{71} (A_{61} / E_{61}) [(A_{71} / E_{71}) / (A_{61} / E_{61})]$$

In this expression, E refers to the total level of employment in the economy and subscripts are years. The number of accountants in 1971 (A_{71}) is the product of total employment in 1971 (E_{71}), the 1961 ratio of accountants to total employees (A_{61}/E_{61}) and the economy-wide ratio of accountants to employment in 1971 and 1961. If the ratio of accountants to all employees had remained constant between 1961 and 1971, the first part of the expression alone would give the correct answer. However, the ratio A/E may change and if it does, the term in the square bracket becomes relevant.

Let $G_A = [(A_{71} / E_{71}) / (A_{61} / E_{61})]$.

If $(A_{71} / E_{71}) = (A_{61} / E_{61})$; then $G_A = 1$.

The advantage of this decomposition is that it divides the growth in the number of accountants between 1961 and 1971 into two components. The first component is the result of overall employment growth (E_{71}). The second component is G_A; the growth in the ratio of accountants to all employees between 1961 and 1971.

Consider the number of accountants in manufacturing in 1971 (A^M_{71}). We have the actual number of accountants, but we need an estimate of this number in the absence of contracting out. Our estimate relates directly to the expression described above. We assume that the number of accountants in manufacturing will change in proportion to overall manufacturing employment and in proportion to the economy-wide change in accountants per employee. Our estimate of the number of accountants who would be employed in the manufacturing sector in the absence of additional contracting out is the following:

$$A^M_{71} = E^M_{71} (A^M_{61} / E^M_{61}) [G_A]$$

All variables including G_A have been defined above.

Our alternative measure deals not with accountants per employee (A/E) but with accountants per unit of output (A/Q). The methodology, however, remains exactly the same.

In more general terms, the two predicted levels are calculated as follows. The output measure is the following:

$$L_{ijt+1} = Q_{jt+1} (L_{ijt} / Q_{jt}) [(L_{it+1} / Q_{t+1}) / (L_{it} / Q_t)].$$

Lij denotes the level of employment of occupation i in industry j. Q_j refers to output in industry j. Q refers to aggregate output, and t and t+l are time subscripts. The employment measure is given below:

$$L_{ijt+1} = L_{jt+1} (L_{ijt} / L_{jt}) [(L_{it+1} / L_{t+1}) / (L_{it} / L_t)].$$

L_t refers to aggregate employment.

Our first measure assumes that the sum of the respective effects of the substitution of other labour and capital for occupation i workers and technological change on output per occupation i worker is the same in all industries. The second measure, which is less demanding, assumes that the rate of substitution of other labour for occupation i workers is the same in all industries.

If these assumptions do not hold and the intensity of the use of occupation i labour in industry j has risen faster (slower) than the economy-wide average, then our estimate of contracting out will be too low (high). This problem bedevils all of our measures of contracting out.

There are no Canadian studies with which our approach can be compared and we are not aware of studies anywhere that have used the methodology that we have developed. A study that is comparable in some respects to our own is a recent U.S. Bureau of Labor Statistics study by John Tschetter.[1] The following paragraphs provide a comparison of our approach with that of Tschetter.

Tschetter focused on the U.S. manufacturing sector and tried to estimate the extent to which clerical and service occupations have been unbundled. He uses an accounting framework and detailed occupation by industry employment data from 1983 to 1986 to decompose changes in the employment of workers in managerial, professional, clerical and service occupations within manufacturing.

The changes analyzed were the following:

- industry employment growth
- changes in the mix of manufacturing industries

- changes in industry staffing patterns (defined as the within industry employment share of each occupational group).

Our analysis did not take account of the changing industry mix within manufacturing and the other industry groups analyzed, but we did carry out a disaggregated analysis for two-digit industries within manufacturing. In addition, Tschetter found almost no impact of a changing industry mix so that this difference between studies is not an important one.

Tschetter's analysis of the respective effects of industry growth and staffing patterns on employment in service occupations began with the decomposition of the employment change for the ith occupation in jth industry into industry employment growth and industry employment share effects.

$$dL_{ij} / L_{ij} = dL_j / L_j + (dL_{ij} / L_{ij} - dL_j / L_j)$$
$$= dL_j / L_j + ds_{ij} / s_{ij}.$$

The symbol sij is the share of the ith occupational group in the employment of the jth industry.

Tschetter defined unbundling as an absolute decline in the employment of the ith occupational group in the jth industry. This can occur as a result of a decline in industry employment with fixed staffing patterns ($dL_j < 0$) or a decline in the employment share of the ith occupation ($dsij < 0$) or both.

To facilitate comparison with our approach we write Tschetter's decomposition in discrete terms as

$$L_{ijt+1} = L_{ijt} \ \{(L_{jt+1} / L_{jt}) + [(L_{ijt+1} / L_{jt+1}) / (L_{ijt} / L_{jt})] - 1\}).$$

Tschetter would infer unbundling if the terms in the curly brackets sum to less than one. This can be the result of a decline in the absolute size of the jth industry ($L_{jt+1} < L_{jt}$) or a decline in the proportion of the employment of the jth industry accounted for by the ith occupation $[(L_{ijt+1} / L_{jt+1}) \ (L_{ijt} / L_{jt})]$ or both. Holding industry growth constant, any decline in the ith occupation's share of the jth industry's employment is regarded by Tschetter as the unbundling or contracting out of that occupation by that industry.

We believe our approach is superior. Our predicted level of employment for the ith occupation in the jth industry in year t+1 can be written as below:

$$L_{ijt+1} = L_{ijt} \{ (L_{jt+1} / L_{jt}) [(L_{it+1} / L_{t+1}) / (L_{it} / L_t)] \}.$$

We infer contracting out if the expression in the curly brackets is less than one. This implies:

$$[(L_{ijt+1} / L_{ijt}) / (L_{jt+1} / L_{jt}) < [(L_{it+1} / L_{t+1}) / (L_{it} / L_{t})].$$

In the simplest terms, we infer contracting out only if the employment share of the ith occupation in the jth industry grows more slowly (declines faster) than the economy-wide average for that occupation. For example, if the share of janitors in machinery industry employment falls by five percent and the share of janitors in the labour force also falls by five percent, Tschetter would infer unbundling while we would not.

EMPIRICAL RESULTS

Accountants

Table 2 shows the employment of accountants and their employment share by major industry group. Overall, accounting employment grew by a factor of nearly five from 1961 to 1981. The number of accountants in the accounting services industry grew substantially but at a slower rate than total accounting employment. This is reflected in a share decline in SIC 861 for the 1961 to 1971 time period. Between 1971 and 1981, however, SIC 861 grew more rapidly than overall accounting employment.

We analyze contracting out on the basis of our projections of the employment of accountants by industry in the absence of any contracting out. Actual employment levels are subtracted from estimated levels to determine the extent of contracting out. For each of the major industry groups, our estimates of the extent to which accounting services have been contracted out are shown in table 3. Negative numbers indicate that actual employment of accountants exceeded predicted levels. The presence of negative signs is a feature of both approaches to predicting employment levels since both constrain total predicted employment to actual levels.

The data in table 3 do not provide an unambiguous picture of the extent of contracting out since the two measures sometimes provide substantially different results. The strongest support for a hypothesis of contracting out is provided by mines, quarries and oil wells, manufacturing and by transportation, communications and utilities. The output share measures in the first two columns of table 3 suggest that 9800 accounting jobs were contracted out from these sectors between 1961 and 1971 and a further 5500 jobs were contracted out between 1971 and 1981. This amounts to 9.6 percent and 3.3 percent of accountants employed in 1971 and 1981 respectively.

The two-digit level within the manufacturing sector provides greater disaggregation to probe for differences among industries in the extent to which contracting out of services occurs. Estimates of the extent of contracting out

Table 2
Employment by Industry: Accountants (SOC 1171)
(Percentage of Total)

	1961	1971	1981
Agriculture	—	110	235
		(0.1)	(0.2)
Mines, Quarries	777	1,560	3,330
and Oil Wells	(2.6)	(1.5)	(2.2)
Manufacturing	6,279	16,070	19,300
	(20.7)	(15.7)	(12.8)
Construction	891	5,105	7,835
	(2.9)	(5.0)	(5.2)
Transportation,	1,998	4,510	6,890
Communications and Utilities	(6.6)	(4.4)	(4.6)
Trade	2,920	10,205	12,770
	(9.6)	(10.01)	(8.4)
Finance, Insurance and	4,768	27,975	38,250
Real Estate	(15.7)	(27.4)	(25.3)
Services	9,019	25,570	45,345
	(29.7)	(25.0)	(30.0)
Public Administration	3,948	11,085	17,275
	(12.3)	(10.8)	(11.4)
Total	30,400	102,190	151,230
	(100)	(100)	(100)
Accounting Services	8,220	16,510	29,300
(SIC 861)	(27.0)	(16.2)	(19.4)

Source: Census of Canada, *Occupation by Industry*.

Note: Forestry, Fishing and Trapping are omitted in the industry totals above and in subsequent tables.

Table 3
Estimated Contracting Out by Major Industry: Accountants (SOC 1171)
Predicted minus Actual Employment
(Percentage of Base Year Employment)

	E_Q-E		E_E-E	
	1961–71	1971–81	1961–71	1971–81
Agriculture	—	—	—	—
Mines, Quarries and Oil Wells	1,158 (149)	1,546 (99)	569 (73)	−1,071 (69)
Manufacturing	5,916 (94)	2,646 (16)	2,240 (36)	638 (4)
Construction	−2,287 (257)	−874 (17)	−2,434 (273)	−1,079 (21)
Transportation, Communications and Utilities	2,726 (136)	858 (19)	823 (41)	−885 (20)
Trade	−688 (24)	2,852 (28)	−1,234 (42)	2,202 (22)
Finance, Insurance and Real Estate	−11,862 (249)	17,447 (63)	−10,078 (211)	7,945 (28)
Services	6,752 (75)	−8,806 (34)	9,410 (104)	−4,877 (19)
Public Administration	−1,606 (43)	−2,368 (21)	824 (22)	−2,638 (24)

Source: Calculated as described in text.

Note: E_Q and E_E are predicted employment calculated using the output and employment bench-marks respectively as described in text.

of accountants in the two-digit industries are shown in table 4. Consistent with the overall data in table 3, there is substantial contracting out of accounting services. Future empirical work in this area should focus on the determinants of inter-industry differences in contracting out. This point will be pursued in more detail in the conclusion to this chapter.

Security Guards

The employment of security guards by industry and their employment share within each major industry are shown in table 5. These data appear to suggest that contracting out has been of substantial importance. Overall, the proportion of security guards within the service sector (narrowly defined in terms of row eight of table 5) nearly doubled between 1961 and 1981. The security services industry (SIC 855) grew by a factor of nearly six in this twenty-year period while security guard employment less than doubled among the remaining employers.

The contracting out of security guards is examined in more detail in table 6. The largest and least ambiguous numbers of contracted out security guards are found in manufacturing and in transportation, communications and utilities. However, the phenomenon also appears important in mines, quarries and oil wells and in construction and trade as well. The data in table 6 indicate that between 1961 and 1981, the number of contracted out security guards falls in a range between 11,400 and 14,600. This is a large fraction of the total employment levels shown in table 5. For this occupation, the rapid growth of the service sector appears to be the result of contracting out from other sectors.

The very substantial contracting out of security services in the manufacturing sector is confirmed by the data of table 7. Almost without exception, the two-digit manufacturing industries increased the extent of contracting out between 1961 and 1981. The relative extent of this contracting out (as measured by the percentage of base year employment) differs among industries but the fractions are large in almost every case. We recognize the imperfections in our measure of contracting out, but, in the case of security guards, we believe that it provides a useful and unambiguous explanation for service sector growth.

Janitors

The changing industrial distribution of janitors between 1961 and 1981 is shown in table 8. The industrial category Services to Buildings (SIC 898) more than doubled between 1961 and 1971 and nearly doubled between 1971 and 1981. Overall, the number of janitors in this component of the service sector increased by a factor of 4.5 between 1961 and 1981 in comparison to

Table 4
Estimated Contracting Out by Two-Digit Manufacturing: Accountants (SOC 1171)
Predicted minus Actual Employment
(Percentage of Base Year Employment)

	E_Q-E		E_E-E	
	1961–71	1971–81	1961–71	1971–81
Food and Beverages	255	471	33	414
	(32)	(23)	(4)	(20)
Tobacco	54	38	52	23
	(108)	(54)	(104)	(33)
Rubber	–89	247	144	210
	(75)	(47)	(122)	(40)
Leather	–57	72	–35	45
	(108)	(50)	(66)	(31)
Textiles	50	186	–73	84
	(31)	(37)	(45)	(17)
Knitting	–19	45	–45	46
	(70)	(43)	(167)	(44)
Clothing	–154	–384	–150	–373
	(162)	(100)	(158)	(97)
Wood Products	272	–531	68	–602
	(95)	(84)	(24)	(96)
Furniture and Fixtures	–34	–22	–71	15
	(49)	(8)	(103)	(5)
Paper	650	–82	832	–361
	(98)	(7)	(126)	(42)
Printing	–161	84	–44	29
	(58)	(10)	(16)	(3)
Primary Metals	631	–27	500	–170
	(150)	(3)	(118)	(21)
Metal Fabrication	243	–110	6	–35
	(50)	(7)	(1)	(2)
Machinery	384	8	243	–114
	(110)	(1)	(70)	(11)
Transportation Equipment	1,710	361	529	–129
	(304)	(27)	(94)	(10)
Electrical Products	951	470	540	202
	(150)	(30)	(85)	(13)
Non-Metallic Minerals	–249	205	–275	130
	(167)	(29)	(185)	(19)
Petroleum and Coal	303	–100	208	73
	(118)	(20)	(81)	(14)
Chemicals	1,339	499	513	–90
	(213)	(42)	(81)	(8)

Source: As described in text.

Table 5
Employment by Industry: Security Guards (SOC 6115)
(Percentage of Total)

	1961	1971	1981
Agriculture	130	150	200
	(0.4)	(0.3)	(0.2)
Mines, Quarries and Oil Wells	859	685	1,155
	(2.5)	(1.4)	(1.4)
Manufacturing	8,494	6,835	7,220
	(24.9)	(13.6)	(8.8)
Construction	1,400	2,225	2,135
	(4.1)	(4.4)	(2.6)
Transportation, Communications and Utilities	2,890	2,675	2,775
	(8.5)	(5.3)	(3.4)
Trade	1,901	2,195	2,995
	(5.6)	(4.4)	(3.7)
Finance, Insurance and Real Estate	625	1,050	2,045
	(1.8)	(2.1)	(2.5)
Services	41,975	8,845	20,565
	(25.9)	(40.8)	(51.3)
Public Administration	8,945	14,025	21,330
	(26.2)	(27.8)	(26.1)
Total	34,089	50,405	81,830
	(100)	(100)	(100)
Security Services (SIC 855)	4,726	12,145	27,180
	(13.9)	(24.1)	(33.2)

Source: Census of Canada, *Occupation by Industry*.

Table 6
Estimated Contracting Out by Major Industry: Security Guards (SOC 6115)
Predicted minus Actual Employment
(Percentage of Base Year Employment)

	E_Q-E		E_E-E	
	1961–71	1971–81	1961–71	1971–81
Agriculture	48	10	–42	–40
	(37)	(7)	(32)	(27)
Mines, Quarries and Oil Wells	683	–255	392	–31
	(80)	(37)	(46)	(5)
Manufacturing	6,707	3,500	4,495	2,400
	(79)	(51)	(53)	(35)
Construction	–209	1,349	–305	1,206
	(15)	(61)	(22)	(54)
Transportation, Communications	2,090	2,503	854	1,265
and Utilities	(72)	(94)	(30)	(47)
Trade	626	864	476	659
	(33)	(39)	(25)	(30)
Finance, Insurance and Real Estate	–88	–75	24	–79
	(14)	(7)	(3)	(8)
Services	–6,133	–8,226	–4,871	–5,056
	(69)	(40)	(55)	(25)
Public Administration	–3,724	330	–1,022	–324
	(42)	(2)	(11)	(2)

Source: As described in text.

Table 7

Estimated Contracting Out by Two-Digit Manufacturing: Security Guards (SOC 6115)

Predicted minus Actual Employment

(Percentage of Base Year Employment)

	E_Q-E		E_E-E	
	1961–71	1971–81	1961–71	1971–81
Food and Beverages	614	377	484	324
	(58)	(47)	(45)	(40)
Tobacco	−1	53	−2	34
	(1)	(66)	(3)	(43)
Rubber	61	118	166	103
	(53)	(87)	(144)	(76)
Leather	−16	78	9	54
	(13)	(71)	(7)	(49)
Textiles	338	197	199	122
	(83)	(67)	(49)	(41)
Knitting	77	−11	46	−11
	(104)	(37)	(62)	(37)
Clothing	43	25	46	26
	(36)	(28)	(38)	(29)
Wood Products	512	611	200	469
	(51)	(65)	(20)	(50)
Furniture and Fixtures	237	30	190	40
	(119)	(38)	(95)	(50)
Paper	223	309	343	38
	(24)	(35)	(37)	(4)
Printing	54	43	83	10
	(39)	(41)	(60)	(10)
Primary Metals	261	323	267	163
	(37)	(40)	(38)	(22)
Metal Fabrication	740	140	525	150
	(138)	(56)	(98)	(60)
Machinery	368	123	318	98
	(130)	(75)	(113)	(59)
Transportation Equipment	1,594	289	610	209
	(154)	(30)	(59)	(21)
Electrical Products	534	199	400	134
	(115)	(66)	(86)	(45)
Non-Metallic Minerals	165	189	142	153
	(54)	(74)	(47)	(60)
Petroleum and Coal	137	6	112	36
	(91)	(8)	(74)	(45)
Chemicals	667	423	332	169
	(117)	(113)	(58)	(45)

Source: As described in text.

Table 8
Employment by Industry: Janitors (SOC 6191)
(Percentage of Total)

	1961	1971	1981
Agriculture	128	310	415
	(0.1)	(0.2)	(0.2)
Mines, Quarries and Oil Wells	818	1,275	1,560
	(0.8)	(0.8)	(0.7)
Manufacturing	10,283	19,320	22,315
	(10.2)	(11.5)	(9.7)
Construction	1,077	2,445	3,265
	(1.1)	(1.5)	(1.4)
Transportation, Communications and Utilities	5,283	6,360	6,525
	(5.3)	(3.8)	(2.8)
Trade	5,758	8,575	12,795
	(5.7)	(5.1)	(5.5)
Finance, Insurance and Real Estate	9,926	12,155	14,160
	(9.9)	(7.3)	(6.1)
Services	56,009	105,110	154,997
	(55.7)	(62.8)	(67.2)
Public Administration	11,245	11,815	14,455
	(11.2)	(7.1)	(6.3)
Total	100,527	167,365	230,485
	(100)	(100)	(100)
Services to Buildings (SIC 898)	9,087	21,130	41,040
	(9.0)	(12.6)	(17.8)

Source: Census Canada, *Occupation by Industry*.

a factor of just over 2 for janitors elsewhere. This disparity in growth rates suggests that growth in this specialized service industry has been a substitute for employing more janitors directly within other industries.

Our measures of estimated contracting out for the major industry groups are shown in table 9. These data confirm that contracting out has been important in transportation, communication and utilities, finance, insurance and real estate and in public administration. In those three industries, the data indicate that the number of janitorial positions contracted out to the service sector between 1961 and 1981 falls in a range[2] between 15,500 and 18,500. If

Table 9
Estimated Contracting Out by Major Industry: Janitors (SOC 6191)
Predicted minus Actual Employment
(Percentage of Base Year Employment)

	E_Q-E		E_E-E	
	1961–71	1971–81	1961–71	1971–81
Agriculture	111	−54	−202	−149
	(87)	(17)	(158)	(48)
Mines, Quarries and Oil Wells	120	−168	−226	124
	(15)	(13)	(28)	(10)
Manufacturing	−1,766	2,858	−5,290	−429
	(17)	(15)	(51)	(2)
Construction	−784	−86	−935	−309
	(73)	(4)	(87)	(13)
Transportation, Communications and Utilities	2,969	3,899	237	1,207
	(56)	(61)	(4)	(19)
Trade	573	−268	−299	−1,305
	(10)	(3)	(5)	(11)
Finance, Insurance and Real Estate	4,197	4,795	5,278	4,168
	(42)	(39)	(53)	(34)
Services	−7,258	−11,680	−3,468	−3,096
	(13)	(11)	(6)	(3)
Public Administration	2,050	704	4,904	−210
	(18)	(6)	(44)	(2)

Source: As described in text.

we assume that all of these positions appear in the data for Services to Buildings, then increased contracting out accounts for somewhere between 50 percent and 60 percent of the employment growth of this service industry between 1961 and 1981.

The disaggregated results for contracting out janitorial services in the manufacturing industries are shown in table 10. These data show that there is little consistent evidence of contracting out within the manufacturing sector. This is particularly the case for the 1961 to 1971 time period. The 1971 to

1981 time period suggests the presence of some contracting out particularly in printing, transportation equipment and chemicals.

APPLICATION TO THE MARKET FOR LEGAL SERVICES

Empirical Measures

In this Section, we will apply the methodology outlined above to the market for lawyers. A separate sub-section for lawyers exists because there is more published empirical and theoretical work on lawyers to compare with our estimates than there is on the other occupations analyzed in this chapter.

Chapter 2 of this study outlines several hypotheses relating to the decision of firms to use various combinations of internal and external services. The results of these decisions in the case of lawyers are reflected in the data showing the employment of lawyers by industry. These data are presented in table 11 for 1961, 1971 and 1981.

We can draw two conclusions from the data of table 11. The proportion of lawyers employed in the public sector increased substantially between 1961 and 1981. As a result, the employment share of the legal services industry (SIC 866) fell from 87.3 percent to 82.7 percent. However, if lawyers in Public Administration are removed from the data, the legal services industry grew from 87.2 percent of private sector employment to 92.1 percent. This is consistent with a small degree of contracting out in the private sector and a substantial degree of internalizing legal services in the public sector.

These conclusions are supported by the results of table 12. These results are based on the two methods of measuring contracting out developed above. There is no clear pattern of contracting out in the private sector. In public administration, however, the data suggest that somewhere between 1,335 and 1,477 legal positions were created to replace work that otherwise would have been contracted out to law firms.

These results support the findings of Pashigian[3] in his study of corporate lawyers in the United States. He found a growth in the absolute number of lawyers in corporate law departments but not at a faster rate than in the legal services industry. He also found that most of the growth in lawyers outside the legal services sector was accounted for by the public and not-for-profit sectors.

Firms with a large in-house legal staff are responding to an information asymmetry common to many professional services. Non-lawyer clients within corporations are at a disadvantage in monitoring the activities of legal professionals. The predominant function of in-house legal counsel should be to monitor the performance of external legal counsel retained by the firm. As

Table 10
Estimated Contracting Out by Two-Digit Manufacturing: Janitors (SOC 6191)
Predicted minus Actual Employment
(Percentage of Base Year Employment)

	E_Q-E		E_E-E	
	1961–71	1971–81	1961–71	1971–81
Food and Beverages	–1,078	–352	–1,436	–751
	(66)	(9)	(76)	(20)
Tobacco	–81	82	–88	32
	(79)	(40)	(86)	(16)
Rubber	–206	212	–73	164
	(132)	(43)	(47)	(33)
Leather	–42	–22	–22	–53
	(34)	(16)	(18)	(38)
Textiles	163	237	–214	53
	(37)	(35)	(48)	(7)
Knitting	42	25	–8	20
	(43)	(23)	(8)	(18)
Clothing	–19	–237	–29	–250
	(5)	(52)	(8)	(55)
Wood Products	–1,024	108	–1,159	–150
	(299)	(7)	(339)	(10)
Furniture and Fixtures	—	3	—	24
		(1)		(8)
Paper	–551	387	–497	–36
	(78)	(26)	(70)	(2)
Printing	–13	513	116	210
	(1)	(50)	(14)	(20)
Primary Metals	–210	116	–510	–274
	(22)	(6)	(53)	(15)
Metal Fabrication	71	–99	–133	–109
	(10)	(9)	(20)	(10)
Machinery	144	26	51	–68
	(42)	(5)	(15)	(12)
Transportation Equipment	67	428	–871	200
	(8)	(19)	(101)	(10)
Electrical Products	213	315	2	138
	(39)	(37)	(0)	(16)
Non-Metallic Minerals	–132	149	–176	59
	(42)	(25)	(56)	(10)
Petroleum and Coal	74	43	36	89
	(47)	(25)	(23)	(52)
Chemicals	578	645	–29	70
	(68)	(58)	(3)	(6)

Source: As described in text.

Table 11
Employment by Industry: Lawyers (SOC 2343)
(Percentage of Total)

	1961	1971	1981
Agriculture	—	—	5
			(–7)
Mines, Quarries and Oil Wells	111	105	265
	(1.0)	(0.6)	(0.8)
Manufacturing	122	145	225
	(1.0)	(0.9)	(0.7)
Construction	—	30	55
		(0.1)	(0.2)
Transportation, Communications and Utilities	160	220	290
	(1.3)	(1.3)	(0.8)
Trade	62	35	125
	(0.5)	(0.2)	(0.4)
Finance, Insurance and Real Estate	215	320	605
	(1.8)	(2.0)	(.18)
Services	10,573	14,075	29,140
	(87.8)	(86.2)	(85.2)
Public Administration	805	1,390	3,480
	(6.7)	(8.5)	(10.2)
Total	12,048	16,320	34,190
	(100)	(100)	(100)
Legal Services (SIC 866)	10,514	13,695	28,290
	(87.3)	(83.9)	(82.7)

Source: Census of Canada, *Occupation by Industry*.

Table 12
Estimated Contracting Out by Major Industry: Lawyers
Predicted versus Actual Employment
(Percentage of Base Year Employment)

	E_Q-E		E_E-E	
	1961–71	1971–81	1961–71	1971–81
Agriculture	—	—	—	—
Mines, Quarries and Oil Wells	45 (41)	–88 (84)	4 (4)	–60 (57)
Manufacturing	20 (16)	65 (45)	–18 (15)	19 (13)
Construction	—	—	—	—
Transportation, Communications and Utilities	4 (3)	266 (121)	–67 (42)	105 (48)
Trade	43 (69)	–46 (131)	33 (53)	–56 (160)
Finance, Insurance and Real Estate	–40 (19)	163 (51)	–32 (15)	109 (34)
Services	561 (5)	433 (3)	586 (6)	946 (7)
Public Administration	–603 (75)	–732 (53)	–475 (59)	–1,002 (72)

Source: As described in text.

Carr and Mathewson[4] pointed out, law firms also monitor their own activities and the extent of this monitoring will be determined partly by external monitoring activities.

External monitoring can substitute for internal monitoring. Carr and Mathewson accept as a stylized fact the contention that a growing proportion of corporate legal work is handled internally. They suggest that vertical integration has occurred thereby reducing the volume of contracted out work.[5] These observations can be assessed in relation to the data of tables 11 and 12.

The limitation of the data in table 2 is that the overall volume of corporate legal work cannot be separated from the non-corporate total. The data on lawyers by industry show the extent of in-house corporate legal work, but there are no comparable data on external corporate lawyers. If we assume that the overall ratio of corporate legal services to all other legal services is constant, then we find a declining relative share of internal lawyers in manufacturing and in transportation, communication and utilities. The Mathewson and Carr observation of an increasing intensity of in-house legal work can be correct only if the total volume of corporate law has declined relative to overall legal services. We are unable to determine this from the occupation by industry data of table 2.

No change in the industrial distribution of lawyers need occur for the Carr and Mathewson monitoring hypothesis to hold. Internal monitoring of external counsel has always been necessary and table 2 shows that there have been substantial numbers of corporate lawyers in each of the Census years. These data suggest only that there is no direct evidence for a growing importance of internal monitoring.

In table 12, there appears to have been a small amount of contracting out of legal work in manufacturing between 1971 and 1981 and somewhat more contracting out in transportation, communications and utilities and in finance, insurance and real estate in the same time period. This conclusion is based on our two assumptions for estimating the number of lawyers in the absence of contracting out. First, the number of lawyers per unit of output grows at the economy-wide rate, and, second, the number of lawyers per employee grows at the economy-wide rate.

In the case of lawyers, these economy-wide rates include lawyers handling non-corporate business in the service sector. If this non-corporate business is increasing more rapidly than corporate business, our methods will over-estimate the number of lawyers in each of the industries in table 12. A resolution of this issue requires data that are not available on the legal service intensity of industry output in the different time periods. On the basis of our data, however, the hypothesis that more internal monitoring of lawyers is occurring does not receive much support.

A further assertion frequently encountered with regard to the employment of lawyers is that the growth of government regulation has spurred the growth of the legal industry. This hypothesis is consistent with the large increase in the number of lawyers between 1961 and 1981, but, again, we cannot separate out corporate legal services. The data show a declining share of lawyers in manufacturing, for example, but the sector could be spending substantially more on external legal services as a response to regulation. This possibility would require an increase in contracting out and would contribute to a growing corporate share of the legal services industry.

Employment of Patent and Trademark Agents

To pursue the issue of contracting out legal services in more detail, we collected data on lawyers working as patent and trademark agents from the Patent and Trademark Institute of Canada (PTIC). Their records allowed us to classify members as employees of industrial corporations or as members of legal firms specializing in the area of intellectual property. The basic data on patent and trademark agents at ten year intervals from 1956 to 1986 are presented in table 13. The distribution of the PTIC members employed by industrial corporations is shown in table 14.

The data in table 13 show a decline in the ratio of fellows and associates of the PTIC employed by industrial companies relative to fellows and associates employed by law firms between 1956 and 1986. This is consistent with the view that contracting out of this type of specialized legal work has increased relative to the base period. Table 14 shows the increasing importance of the electrical and electronics industries in the industrial employment of PTIC members and the corresponding relative decline of the chemical industries.

CONCLUSIONS

The measures of contracting out derived above are best suited to occupational classifications for which there is a corresponding industry classification. This enables the investigator to compare employment in the using industries with employment in the industry to which specialized outside contractors would be assigned. Not all occupational categories meet these requirements.

Our results hinge on the validity of the assumption that the rate of change in the intensity of use of the ith occupation is the same in all industries. If this is not the case and a sector, say manufacturing, has become a relatively less intensive user of, say security guards, we will infer contracting out when there has, in fact, been none. The results reported in this Section are insuffi-

Table 13
Membership in the Patent and Trademark Institute of Canada

	1956	1966	1976	1986
1. Fellows	56	110	173	226
2. Associates	35	67	127	78
3. Fellows Employed by Industrial Corporations	11	22	26	28
4. Associates Employed by Industrial Corporations	10	18	23	20
5. 1+2	91	177	300	304
6. 3+4	21	40	49	48
7. 6/5	.231	.225	.163	.158
8. 3/1	.196	.200	.150	.124
9. 4/2	.286	.269	.181	.256
10. Number of Corporations	16	21	24	22

Source: PTIC annual reports.

Notes: Fellows have been patent or trademark agents for five years and have been associates for two years. Associates have been patent or trademark agents for two years. Both Fellows and Associates must be principally occupied as patent or trademark agents.

Table 14
Employment of PTIC Members by Industry

	1956	1966	1976	1986
Chemical and Allied Industries	9	17	22	13
Electrical and Electronic	9	14	16	21
Resource Industries	1	4	7	8
Other	3	3	3	6
Total	22	38	48	48

Source: PTIC annual reports.

cient by themselves to support unambiguous inferences regarding contracting out.

Insofar as the results themselves are concerned, several characteristics are worthy of note. First, estimated rates of contracting out vary from occupation to occupation and from period to period. In the case of the manufacturing sector, for example, we observe the following:

Occupation	Contracting out as a percentage of employment	
	1961-1971	1971-1981
Accountants	36	4
Security Guards	53	35
Janitors	-51	-2

Within the manufacturing sector we observe significant contracting out of one occupation, modest contracting out of another and contracting in in the third. Contrary to the conventional view, the rate of contracting out is lower in the seventies than in the sixties.

The estimated rate of contracting out also varies across industries within occupations. In the case of janitors, for example, we observe the following:

Industry	Contracting out as a percentage of janitorial employment	
	1961-1971	1971-1981
Manufacturing	-51	-2
Construction	-87	-13
Transportation, Storage and Communication	4	19
Finance, Insurance and Real Estate	53	54

With respect to janitors we find some industries massively contracting in, some heavily contracting out and others modestly contracting out. Again these tendencies differ in magnitude (but not in direction in this case) between subperiods.

These results suggest that the rate of contracting out is determined by the interaction of industry and occupational characteristics and that the nature of this interaction varies over time. There is no single determining factor at work.

One frequently encountered hypothesis is that much contracting out occurs in response to union wage rates and work rules. This issue is discussed in chapter 6 of this study but a preliminary assessment can be made on the basis of the contracting out estimates in this chapter. Accountants are not members of most bargaining units, so we would not expect industry unionization to be a determining factor explaining the contracting out of accounting services. Janitors and security guards, however, are typically members of bargaining units and it may be the case that the extent to which their services are contracted out can be related to industry unionization ratios. Our analysis is based on our measure of contracting out and the unionization rate for manufacturing industries at the two-digit level.

We recognize that the true relationship between contracting out and unionization cannot be established through simple cross-tabulations. There are many factors influencing contracting out and the influence of unionism should be assessed in a complete model. However, for the purposes of this study, we have limited our analysis to the simple bivariate relationship between unionization and contracting out.

Tables 15 and 16 show the relationship between contracting out and unionization for security guards and for janitors. The measure of contracting out is (E_E-E) from tables 7 and 10. For each occupation, the number of contracted out jobs between 1961 and 1981 is expressed as a fraction of the 1961 benchmark level of employment in that occupation.

For security guards, every two-digit manufacturing industry engaged in contracting out between 1961 and 1981. Table 15 tabulates data for the five industries with the largest proportion of contracting out and the five industries with the least contracting out. The final column shows the unionization ratio for each industry. These data show that there may be a weak bivariate relationship between contracting out and unionization. The industry with the highest unionization ratio engaged in the most contracting out, while the industries with the lowest unionization ratios (knitting and leather) were among the industries with the least contracting out. There are obvious contradictions, however, and the average unionization rate for the five industries with the most contracting out exceeds that of the industries with the least contracting out by only a small margin.

Table 15
Contracting Out and Unionization: Security Guards

Industries with the Largest Proportion of Contracting Out	Extent of Contracting Out Between 1961 and 1981 (percent of 1961 employment)	Unionization Ratio, 1971
Rubber	234	92
Machinery	148	38
Metal Fabrication	126	45
Electrical Products	115	53
Furniture and Fixtures	115	31
Average for Top Five	148	52
Industries with the Least Contracting Out		
Paper	42	67
Tobacco	46	73
Knitting	47	15
Leather	50	34
Clothing	60	54
Average for Bottom Five	49	49

Sources: Table 10 and Labour Canada, *Industrial and Geographic Distribution of Union Members in Canada*, 1971.

Table 16

Contracting Out and Unionization: Janitors

Industries with the Largest Proportion of Contracting Out	Extent of Contracting Out Between 1961 and 1981 (percent of 1961 employment)	Unionization Ratio, 1971
Petroleum	79	24
Rubber	58	92
Printing	39	32
Electrical Products	25	53
Knitting	12	15
Average for Top Five	43	43
Industries with the Least Contracting Out		
Wood Products	–382	46
Food and Beverages	–115	42
Primary Metals	–81	58
Transportation Equipment	–78	69
Clothing	–76	54
Average for Bottom Five	–146	54

Sources: Table 10 and Labour Canada, *Industrial and Geographic Distribution of Union Members in Canada*, 1971.

The data in table 16 provide a classification of contracting out of janitors by industries with differing unionization ratios. In manufacturing as a whole, substantial contracting in persists during this time period as the data in table 9 show. No apparent relationship between high unionization rates and contracting out exists. In fact, we find that the industries with higher unionization rates were contracting in.

NOTES

1. See John Tschetter, "Producer services industries: Why are they growing so fast?" U.S. Bureau of Labor Statistics, September, 1987. This paper was drawn to our attention after we completed the first draft of our own work.
2. The output measure provides the higher estimate.
3. B. Peter Pashigian, "Regulation, Preventive Law, and the Duties of Attorneys," in W.J. Carney (ed.), *The Changing Role of the Corporate Attorney*, (Toronto: Lexington Books, 1982), pp. 3-46.
4. J. Carr and F. Mathewson, "The Economics of the Legal Organization of Firms" (Mimeo, University of Toronto, 1987).
5. Carr and Mathewson, p. 3.

Chapter 4

MEASURES OF VERTICAL SPECIALIZATION DERIVED FROM THE CENSUS OF MANUFACTURES[1]

INTRODUCTION

The value added to sales (or shipments) ratio, VA/S, has been widely used as an indicator of the degree of vertical integration in manufacturing establishments or industries for a number of years (Adelman, 1951). Value added is defined as the value of shipments minus the cost of purchased material and energy inputs. It is the amount paid for the capital and labour required to transform the "raw" materials into the "finished" product which is then sold to end users, downstream processors or merchandisers who transform it further.

Over time, an increase in VA/S implies that the plant, firm or industry concerned has become more vertically integrated, that is, that it encompasses more stages of production. A decrease in VA/S implies that the plant or industry involved is specializing vertically, that is, is spanning fewer stages of production.

To illustrate the calculation of VA/S, suppose initially that the annual shipments of a manufacturing plant are valued at $200 and the cost of fuel and materials purchased is $100. Value added is $100 and VA/S is 0.5.

Suppose this plant integrates backward. That is, materials formerly purchased from an upstream supplier are now made within the plant. Let the value of the materials now made rather than bought be $20. Materials purchases now amount to $80. Value added is $120 and VA/S increases to 0.6.

Backward disintegration involves the purchase of some material inputs formerly made within the plant from an upstream supplier. The plant is effectively specializing in the later stages of production. Suppose the value of the materials concerned is $20. Value added declines to $80 and VA/S to 0.4

PROBLEMS OF INTERPRETATION

Cross-Sectional Comparisons

The value added to shipments ratio from the Census of Manufactures is useful for measuring changes in the degree of vertical integration of a plant or industry over time. It is not a good indicator of inter-industry differences in vertical integration at a given time. Given the same amount of value adding activity, an industry specialized to the early stages of production will have a higher VA/S than an industry (or plant or firm) specialized to the later stages of production.

Asymmetry Between Backward and Forward Integration

Using the example in the first section of this chapter, we can demonstrate that a given percentage change in value adding activity has a different effect on VA/S depending on whether it involves upstream or downstream suppliers or customers. Suppose that downstream integration occurs. Additional processing in the amount of $20 which had been done elsewhere is now done in the plant in question. Shipments are now valued at $220. Value added becomes $120 and VA/S is 0.55. Thus a 20 per cent increase in value adding activity results in a 10 per cent increase in VA/S if the integration involved is backward and 5 per cent if it is forward.

A similar asymmetry prevails in the case of disintegration (vertical specialization). If value adding activity in the amount of $20 is shifted to downstream customers VA/S falls to 0.44 (80/180). If it is shifted to upstream suppliers VA/S falls to 0.4 (80/200).

One implication of this asymmetry is that VA/S will fall if an industry migrates to a later stage of the production process and it may change in any direction if this migration is accompanied by increased integration.

Defining Value Added

Value added is defined implicitly as the difference between the respective values of shipments of product and purchases of material inputs and fuel. In some cases it is unclear what a purchased material input is. An example is payments to piece-rate workers. These payments could be treated as salary or hourly wages and thus included in value added, or they could be treated as payments to upstream supplies of materials. The issue of whether piece rate workers are employees also arises in connection with the definition of the firm. Cheung (1983) concluded that there is no definitive answer to this question. Eccles (1982) argued that there is a continuum of piece-rate arrangements. At one end is a piece rate worker who supplies his own tools and materials and sells to more than one customer either at a given point in time or over a relatively short period of time. This worker is a supplier rather than an employee. At the other extreme is a piece rate worker who uses tools and materials supplied by the customer and works exclusively for that customer over extended periods of time. This individual is an employee. There is no agreement on the intermediate point at which an employee becomes an independent input supplier.

The Census of Manufactures treats payments to "on-site" piece workers as wages of employees (part of value-added) and payments to "off-site" piece workers as purchased materials. In the case of manufacturing establishments, this is a reasonable decision because on-site workers are probably using tools and materials provided by the customer and working exclusively for one customer. For other industries such as construction or transportation the distinction between on-site and off-site workers would not be helpful.

There are further difficulties in applying this type of reasoning to workers in service occupations. In some cases, janitorial services for example, a piece-rate is difficult to define and few tools or materials are involved. In this case, the definition of an employee depends on the duration and exclusivity of the arrangement.

The Census of Manufactures does not collect information on purchased service inputs. Thus, payments for service inputs such as those provided by janitors or lawyers is included in value added regardless of whether the individuals involved are deemed to be employees or not. A manufacturing plant which replaces a salaried janitor with an outside janitorial services contractor would report the same shipments and approximately the same fuel and materials purchases. Value added (shipments minus fuel and materials) is unchanged as is VA/S. The wages and salaries to value added ratio, W/VA, declines.[2]

The story is slightly different in the case of a downstream outside supplier. Examples are somewhat difficult to find. One possibility is that promotional activities formerly performed by the manufacturer are now performed by wholesalers, jobbers or retailers. The manufacturer's wages and salaries, value added and shipments all fall. Under normal conditions, this forward disintegration will also result in decreases in both VA/S and W/VA.[3]

As far as manufacturing establishments are concerned, VA/S is not a useful indicator of changes in the degree of backward integration where service inputs are involved. VA/S continues to be a useful indicator of changes in the degree of forward integration involving service inputs, although this may occur less often. The ratio of wages and salaries to value added, W/VA is a potential indicator of changes in the degree of vertical integration, both forward and backward, involving service inputs. This ratio may also vary for reasons unrelated to the degree of integration. A more refined measure would eliminate payments for production inputs (payments to capital and production workers) from both the numerator and denominator.

Variation in Profits

Since profit or, more broadly, quasi-rent is a component of value added, the latter will vary with profit rates over the business cycle. This variation should be most pronounced in industries employing relatively large amounts of fixed capital. In these industries, VA/S will be higher at the peak of the cycle when capacity utilization is high than at the trough.

In order to make correct inferences regarding secular rates of change in VA/S, cyclical factors must be held constant either by comparing similar points in the business cycle or by removing (by regression analysis) the influence of capacity utilization. Another alternative adopted by Wilder and Tucker (1977) is to exclude before tax profits from value added. This removes the effects of both cyclical and secular changes in profit rates on value added. But it does so at the cost of eliminating returns to equity from value added. This creates additional problems if leverage ratios change, and it does not ameliorate other potentially more severe measurement problems. For example, nominal rates of interest can also vary over the business cycle due to variations in the anticipated rate of inflation.

Changes in Relative Prices and Differential Rates of Technical Change

If we define VA/S as

$$S_V = P_V V / (P_V V + P_I I)$$

then

$$d(VA/S) / VA/S = (1-S_V) \{[(dP_V / P_V) + (dV / V)] - [(dP_I / P_I) + (dI / I)]\}.$$

P_V equals the price per unit of the value adding factor. V equals the units of the value adding factor per unit of output.

P_I equals the price per unit of the purchased input; and I equals units of the purchased input per unit of output.

It is evident from this expression that an increase in the relative price of the value adding factor $[(dP_V/P_V) - (dP_I/P_I) > 0]$ increases VA/S and vice versa without any changes in make or buy policy. As we will demonstrate, this occurred in the petroleum refining industry where increases in the price of crude oil reduced VA/S in that industry by some 40 percent since 1972.

Similarly, factor saving technological change may occur at different rates for the purchased and value adding inputs ($dV/V \neq dI/I$) thus changing VA/S. Some studies of technological change in the seventies found that in some industries it was energy saving and capital using. By itself this would imply dI/I < 0, dV/V > 0 with VA/S increasing.

Level of Measurement

Changes in VA/S can be measured at the plant, firm or industry level. Changes in the degree of vertical integration can have a different effect on VA/S depending on the level at which the latter is measured.

Consider a production process with two stages I and II. Two plants A and B initially perform both stages; they are fully integrated. If value added at each stage is $50, then the shipments of each plant are valued at $100 and industry shipments at $200. VA/S is 1 for each plant for the industry and for the firm(s) owning the plants (provided this is their only activity).

Suppose full vertical specialization (disintegration) occurs at the plant level. Plant A specializes at stage I and B at stage II. These shipments of plant A are worth $100 and VA/S is 1. The shipments of B are worth $200 and VA/S falls to 0.5. Measured at the industry level (netting out intra-industry shipments) VA/S remains at 1. For a two plant firm (netting out intra-firm shipments) VA/S remains at 1. Measured as a weighted average of plant VA to S ratios, which is what the Census of Manufactures provides, VA/S is 0.67 (200/300).

The same amount of specialization would yield a different census VA/S value if either of the newly specialized plants were assigned to a different industry for statistical purposes or, more importantly, if the vertical specialization were international in nature. Suppose, for example, that plants A and B are each specialized to stage II and that stage I is performed abroad. If domestic industry value added remains at $200, then industry shipments are valued at $400—half of which is exported. Domestic industry VA/S drops to 0.5. If the foreign stage I producers are owned by the same firm as the domestic plants, the VA to S ratio of this (multinational) firm remains at 1.

Two points are relevant here. First, the effect of vertical specialization (or integration) on VA/S depends on whether it is carried out on an intra-industry, inter-industry or international basis. Second VA to S ratios can differ markedly depending on whether they are calculated for plants, firms or industries.

Firm level VA to S ratios indicate how many stages of production are under common ownership; plant level VA to S ratios indicate how many successive stages of production are conducted in the same establishment. For this study, the important question is whether individual establishments (rather than firms) are becoming more or less specialized by stage of production.

Horizontal versus Vertical Specialization

An alternative form of specialization which has generated considerable interest is horizontal specialization (Baldwin and Gorecki, 1983). In manufacturing, it involves individual plants' concentration on production of a narrow (or narrower) range of product lines. It often—but not necessarily—causes a reduction in the number of product lines sold by individual firms.

Horizontal specialization can occur both domestically and internationally. Domestically it could involve both intra-firm and inter-firm specialization. When intra-firm specialization occurs in multiplant firms, individual plants are allocated responsibilities for supplying the firm's requirements for particular product lines. Inter-firm specialization implies either that some firms cease producing *and selling* particular product lines or that they cease producing them and rely on other firms for their supplies.

Purely domestic specialization may be insufficient to exhaust the economies of large batch size. Economies will not be exhausted if the optimal batch size is large relative to the domestic market, or if inter-firm specialization agreements are especially costly to negotiate and enforce. Further specialization can then occur internationally. Domestic plants can concentrate on particular product lines which export output in excess of domestic requirements. Remaining product lines can be imported. Thus, trade liberalization will facilitate further specialization—both horizontal and vertical. To some authors, Harris and Cox (1983), for example, trade liberalization is also important because it *forces* specialization. These authors assume firms will not take advantage of the domestic opportunities for specialization unless a reduction in the landed price of competing imports compels it.

Depending on how it is measured, the VA to S ratio may be affected by horizontal integration or disintegration. Suppose a manufacturing plant specializes in one of its two product lines. The second product line is purchased from other firms. The reshipment of the second product line reduces the industry VA:S ratio.

Canadian data allow both the separation of the respective effects of changes in vertical and horizontal integration and the calculation of a crude measure of horizontal integration. The Census of Manufactures distinguishes between shipments of goods of own manufacture and shipments of goods purchased for resale. The ratio of value added by manufacture to shipments of goods of own manufacture reflects the degree of vertical integration. The ratio of shipments of goods of own manufacture to total shipments is a rough indicator of the degree of horizontal integration. It is a rough indicator because it includes only those product lines which are purchased and reshipped from manufacturing establishments. Product lines going to separate warehouses or directly to wholesalers or retail dealers (such as automobiles shipped from U.S. plants) would not be covered.

ASSESSING ALTERNATIVE MEASURES OF INTEGRATION

A measure of vertical integration involving material inputs is the following:

RVM = Value added by manufacture/value of shipments of goods and services of own manufacture.

This ratio is an increasing function of the degree of vertical integration. The marginal effect of a change in the degree of integration on RVM depends on whether it is forward or backward. This ratio will also vary with the rate of capacity utilization, especially in capital intensive industries. It is also affected by changes in the respective relative prices of important inputs.

A measure of vertical integration involving service inputs is the following:

RVS = Non-production wages and salaries/total value added minus payments to capital and production wages.

This ratio is an increasing function of the degree of vertical integration in nonmaterial inputs. The marginal effect of a change in the degree of integration on RVS depends on whether upstream or downstream suppliers are involved. Changes in the degree of integration involving services performed in offices *not* located in manufacturing establishments will not change the value of RVS.

A measure of horizontal integration is the following:

RH = Shipments of goods of own manufacture/total shipments and other revenue

This ratio is an increasing function of the degree of horizontal integration. Horizontal specialization will not result in a decrease in this ratio if it does not involve cross-shipment of finished goods among manufacturing plants. The effect of specialization involving shipments direct to wholesalers or retailers will not be reflected in RH.

EMPIRICAL EVIDENCE

The RVM

The ratio of value added to shipments for all manufacturing in Canada between 1917 and 1984 is reported in table 17. The same ratio calculated annually over the period 1961 to 1984 is reported in table 18. Both tables show no discernible trend in RVM prior to 1970 and a consistent decline thereafter.

Table 17

The Value Added to Shipments Ratio in Manufacturing, 1917-1984

Year	RVM
1917	.454
1921	.452
1926	.421
1931	.490
1936	.430
1941	.429
1946	.431
1951	.423
1956	.444
1961	.445
1966	.438
1971	.432
1976	.406
1981	.388
1984	.385

Sources: Statistics Canada, 31-203.

Table 18

The Value Added to Shipments Ratio in Manufacturing, 1961-1984

Year	RVM	Year	RVM
1961	.445	1973	.431
1962	.443	1974	.426
1963	.438	1975	.408
1964	.439	1976	.406
1965	.440	1977	.405
1966	.438	1978	.400
1967	.437	1979	.398
1968	.436	1980	.392
1969	.438	1981	.388
1970	.432	1982	.367
1971	.432	1983	.378
1972	.432	1984	.385

Source: Statistics Canada, 31-203.

Note: The data are value added in manufacturing and shipments of goods of own manufacture.

Table 19
Value Added to Shipments Ratio in Manufacturing, 1954-1984

	1954	1964	1974	1984	84/74	84/64
Food and Beverage	.332	.336	.302	.325	1.08	0.97
Tobacco and Products	.353	.390	.429	.493	1.15	1.26
Rubber Products	.560	.512	.525	.494	0.94	0.96
Leather Products	.496	.499	.493	.506	1.03	1.01
Textiles	.430	.450	.457	.441	0.96	0.98
Clothing	.473	.468	.479	.517	1.08	1.10
Wood Products	.456	.445	.428	.432	1.01	0.97
Furniture and Fixtures	.524	.506	.513	.520	1.01	1.03
Paper and Allied	.492	.479	.506	.430	0.85	0.90
Printing and Publishing	.666	.676	.657	.629	0.96	0.93
Fabricated Metals	.550	.493	.520	.478	0.92	0.97
Machinery	.551	.502	.498	.509	1.02	1.01
Transportation Equipment	.409	.381	.346	.326	0.94	0.86
Electrical Equipment	.536	.513	.510	.521	1.02	1.02
Non-Metallic Minerals	.590	.559	.568	.510	0.90	0.91
Refined Petroleum and Coal	.351	.202	.187	.112	0.60	0.55
Chemical and Allied	.509	.528	.507	.403	0.79	0.76
Miscellaneous Manufacturing	.591	.553	.538	.511	0.95	0.92
All Manufacturing Industries (1964 Shipment Weights)	.455	.438	.429	.409	0.95	0.93
All Manufacturing Industries (1964 Shipment Weights, Refined Petroleum held at its 1974 value)	.446	.438	.429	.412	0.96	0.94

Source: Statistics Canada, 31-203.

As the industry RVM values reported in Table 19 indicate, the recent decline in this ratio is not common to all manufacturing industries. Between 1974 and 1984, RVM rose in eight industries and declined in eleven. The largest percentage and absolute decline occurred in petroleum refining. This is a result of large increases in the price of crude oil after 1972.

Examination of table 19 reveals that the behaviour of RVM for the manufacturing sector recently may be the result of the large decline in RVM in petroleum refining and related industries, such as chemicals. Increases in the relative importance of industries with less than average RVM values, such as transportation equipment, may also affect RVM's behaviour. Cyclical factors may also have played a role.

In order to eliminate the effect of changes in industry mix on RVM, the latter is recalculated using 1964 shipment weights. The results are reported in table 19. With current period weights (table 18) RVM falls 4.1 percentage (9.6 percent) between 1974 and 1984. With 1964 weights the decline in RVM over this period is two points or 4.7 percent.

The impact of higher crude oil price on RVM in petroleum and thus on RVM in manufacturing can be eliminated by holding RVM in petroleum constant at its 1974 value. The effect of this is to raise the (1964 weighted) 1984 value of RVM for manufacturing by .3 percentage points. The effect is small because petroleum refining accounted for a relatively small proportion (4.6 percent) of manufacturing shipments in 1964. With RVM in petroleum refining held at its 1974 value and with 1964 shipment weights, RVM for manufacturing declines by 1.7 percentage points (4 percent) between 1974 and 1984 implying an annual rate of decline of 0.4 percent.

The secular and cyclical components of the 1964 weighted values of RVM are determined by regressing RVM on a time trend and the rate of capacity utilization in manufacturing. The coefficient of the trend variable is negative and significant at the 99 percent level. The coefficient of capacity utilization is positive (as expected) but significant only at the 80 percent level.

The RVS

The ratio of administrative wages and salaries to residual value added may provide some indication of changes in the degree of vertical integration with respect to service inputs over time. Residual value added is defined as total value added minus payments to capital (rents and quasi-rent) and production wages. Correctly measured, residual value added should include payments for non- material inputs in addition to administrative (non- production) wages and salaries. Contracting out should reduce administrative wages and salaries, leave residual value added unchanged and reduce the ratio of the former to the latter.

We define RVS the following way:

RVS = WA/(VA - K - WP).

K = (C/SF)S.

C = operating profit, depreciation, depletion, amortization of deferred charges and intangibles, long and short-term interest expense, exploration and development charged to current expenses and land and lease acquisition (Statistics Canada 61-003).

SF = Sales of goods and services (Statistics Canada, 61-003)

S = Shipments and other revenue (Statistics Canada, 31-203)

WA = Non-production employee wages and salaries (Statistics Canada, 31-203)

WP = Production employee wages and salaries

VA = Total value added.

The calculation and use of RVS involves two crucial assumptions. The first is that C/SF calculated from the Corporate Financial Statistics is an accurate estimate of payments to capital. The second is that value added minus payments to capital and production wages is essentially composed of payments for internally and externally procured service inputs.

Calculated values of RVS for the manufacturing sector for the period 1962 to 1984 together with C/SF are reported in table 20. There is no trend evident in RVS. Its average values for the periods 1962 to 1966 and 1980 to 1984 are 41.9 and 41.3 respectively. By this measure, there has been no vertical integration involving service inputs. Again, disaggregation or the calculation of a fixed weight index may yield different results.

RH

The ratio of shipments of goods of own manufacture to total shipments and other revenue, RH, in the manufacturing sector from 1961 to 1984 is reported in table 21. RH appears to have been subject to a modest secular decline. Its average value between 1961 and 1965 is .909 and between 1980 and 1984 is .873. Much of this decline appears to have been the result of the transportation equipment industry specialization. RH, averaged over the first and last five years of the series, fell by 15.5 percentage points or 17.4 percent.[4] The reverse appears to have occurred in the Machinery industry where RH increased by 6.7 percentage points or 8.7 percent.

CONCLUSIONS

The Census of Manufactures can be used to derive measures of vertical specialization with respect to either material or service inputs; it can also be used to derive measures of horizontal specialization. These measures show a clear tendency toward vertical specialization in relation to material inputs in many Canadian industries and in the entire manufacturing sector over the last twenty years. Horizontal specialization, as measured here, has been confined largely to the transportation equipment industry. The measure of vertical specialization with regard to service inputs derived in this Section shows no tendency in this direction.

Table 20

Ratio of Administrative Wages to Residual Value Added in Manufacturing, 1962-1984

Year	C/SF* (x100)	RVS (x 100)
1961	—	—
1962	9.8	42.2
1963	10.4	43.1
1964	10.6	41.9
1965	10.5	41.3
1966	9.8	41.1
1967	9.0	41.2
1968	9.1	40.9
1969	9.0	38.5
1970	8.0	41.1
1971	8.5	41.1
1972	10.2	43.4
1973	11.3	42.4
1974	11.8	40.0
1975	10.6	42.6
1976	9.4	41.7
1977	9.5	39.2
1978	10.5	41.1
1979	11.3	40.6
1980	11.6	43.1
1981	10.5	40.9
1982	8.2	42.8
1983	9.6	41.0
1984	10.5	38.9
1985	9.7	—

Sources: As indicated in the text.

Note: *C/SF linked in 1970 using the ratio of the old to the new survey value.

Table 21
Shipments of Goods of Own Manufacture/Shipments and Other Revenue, 1961-1984

Year	Manufacturing	Transportation Equipment	Machinery
1961	.913	.857	.779
1962	.913	.888	.767
1963	.915	.916	.784
1964	.906	.909	.777
1965	.900	.875	.773
1966	.894	.850	.775
1967	.882	.800	.774
1968	.883	.799	.752
1969	.881	.814	.771
1970	.877	.789	.757
1971	.875	.768	.828
1972	.873	.756	.832
1973	.870	.744	.819
1974	.868	.724	.817
1975	.866	.714	.823
1976	.866	.709	.822
1977	.862	.684	.823
1978	.866	.711	.835
1979	.862	.698	.826
1980	.870	.719	.828
1981	.874	.731	.838
1982	.876	.743	.832
1983	.876	.738	.861
1984	.871	.739	.858

Source: Statistics Canada, 31-203.

NOTES

1. Results of the Census of Manufactures are published annually in Statistics Canada, *Manufacturing Industries of Canada: National and Provincial Areas*, Catalogue Number 31-203. It is collected on an establishment basis and, as we note in the text, is of limited use in measuring differences in vertical integration at the *firm* level.

2. Contracting-out of head office or warehouse functions to the service sector will not show up in Census of Manufactures data at all if the office or warehouse involved is not located in a manufacturing establishment. Employees of manufacturing companies in separated head offices or other facilities are not counted as manufacturing employees.

3. With down stream integration or disintegration dS = dVA so that

   $d(VA/S)/dVA = (S-VA)/S^2 > 0$

   Similarly, dW = dVA so that

   $d(W/VA)/dW = (VA-W)/VA^2 > 0$

4. The increase in the relative importance of the Transportation Equipment industry together with the decrease in RH in that industry have the effect of reducing RH in manufacturing by .018 or 45 per cent of the observed decrease.

Chapter 5

MEASURES OF VERTICAL SPECIALIZATION DERIVED FROM THE INPUT-OUTPUT TABLE

INTRODUCTION

The use matrix of the input-output table provides detailed information on the inputs purchased by each industry from other industries. This information can be used to calculate some measures of the change in the degree of vertical integration by industry over time.

USING THE INPUT-OUTPUT TABLE

Input-output based measures of vertical integration reflect changes in vertical integration by establishments rather than firms. That is, the use matrix remains unchanged when an oil refiner purchases a crude oil producer.

The use matrix can be employed to measure vertical specialization involving the substitution of intermediate goods or services purchased from other establishments for those formerly produced within a particular establishment. Service inputs provide some good examples. The business services industry (row 84, aggregation M) includes (i) services to business management (ii) advertising services (iii) data processing equipment rentals and (iv) other services to businesses and persons.

The subgroup services to business management includes accountants, lawyers, and management consultants. If the firms in a given industry provide these services for themselves, much of the cost would appear as wages and salaries (row 97) for that industry. Replacement of in-house personnel with outside suppliers should result in an increase in the value of purchases from business services and a decrease in wages and salaries, other things being equal.

Another example is the personal and miscellaneous services commodity input category (row 89, aggregation M). It includes (i) personal services (ii) photographic services (iii) services to buildings and dwellings (iv) rentals of autos, trucks, construction and other machinery and (v) trade association dues. The subgroup services to buildings and dwellings includes security guard and janitorial service contractors. If janitorial services are contracted out by firms in a particular industry, industry wages and salaries should decline while purchases of services to buildings and dwellings should increase.

Changes in the degree of integration involving these two classes of service inputs can be measured on an industry basis by calculating the ratio of purchases of either group of services by each industry to industry wages and salaries at various times. For business services, we use this definition:

RVSBl = (purchases of business services)/(wages and salaries + supplementary labour income).

The numerator of RVSBl is taken from row 84 of the use matrix (aggregation M). The denominator is the sum of rows 97 and 98. RVSBl can be calculated annually for 33 industries from 1961 to 1981.

Statistics Canada also calculates and publishes a constant dollar use matrix. The matrix is calculated by deflating all input categories and final output by their respective price indexes. The residual is real value added or GDP. GDP includes income of unincorporated business and other operating surplus in addition to labour income. Changes in the constant dollar values of inputs and value added over time reflect changes in physical quantities of inputs used. The effects of relative price changes are washed out. Thus, the ratio of constant dollar purchases of business services to GDP is free of the effects of relative price changes. It comes as close as possible to reflecting changes in the ratio of the number of in-house to outside workers—janitors or lawyers, for example. The problem with the constant dollar ratio is that its denominator, GDP, includes operating profits which are likely to vary cyclically. Consequently, the ratio of business service purchases to GDP may rise during a cyclical contraction (such as between 1981 and 1982) simply because profits have fallen.

With both its advantages and disadvantages in mind, we use the following definition:

RVSB2 = (Purchases of business services in 1971 prices)/(GDP in 1971 prices).

Calculated values of the ratio RSVBl are reported for 33 industries and the entire manufacturing sector for the years 1961, 1971 and 1981 in table 22. Table 23 shows the number of industries in which the ratio of business services to wages and salaries increased or decreased between 1961 and 1981 and between 1971 and 1981. Values of the ratio RVSB2 are reported in table

Table 22
Purchase of Business Services: Wages, Salaries and Supplementary Labour Income in Current Dollars (RSVB1) by Industry, 1961, 1971, 1981 (x 100)

	1961	1971	1981	81/61*	81/71*
Agriculture	1.41	2.26	3.52	4.6	4.4
Forestry	1.26	1.04	0.98	–1.3	–0.6
Fishing and Trapping	0.75	0.77	0.56	–1.5	–3.2
Metal Mines	4.37	6.32	8.67	3.4	3.2
Mineral Fuels	24.60	48.33	31.92	1.3	–4.1
Non-Metal Mines	4.27	3.85	4.83	0.7	2.3
Mining Services	2.98	6.07	7.13	4.4	1.5
Food and Beverage	4.18	3.13	3.50	–0.9	1.1
Tobacco Products	4.76	4.12	4.35	–0.5	0.5
Rubber and Plastic	2.25	4.30	3.50	2.2	–2.1
Leather	1.55	2.16	2.49	2.4	1.4
Textiles	1.61	2.88	3.13	3.3	0.8
Knitting Mills	2.44	1.72	2.03	–0.9	1.7
Clothing Industries	1.27	1.83	2.08	2.5	1.3
Wood	1.14	1.58	1.73	2.1	0.9
Furniture and Fixtures	2.02	2.19	1.87	–0.4	–1.5
Paper and Allied	2.23	2.20	2.26	0.1	0.3
Printing and Publishing	3.00	4.03	4.50	2.0	1.1
Primary Metals	2.71	2.64	2.12	–1.2	–2.2
Metal Fabricating	2.50	2.45	2.59	0.2	0.6
Machinery	2.42	3.37	4.26	2.8	2.3
Transportation Equipment	3.78	14.86	23.10	9.1	4.4
Electrical Products	2.52	2.62	3.24	1.2	2.1
Non-Metallic Minerals	2.13	2.45	2.08	–0.1	–1.6
Petroleum and Coal	3.18	13.03	9.97	5.7	–2.7
Chemicals	5.69	6.26	7.57	1.4	1.9
Miscellaneous Manufacturing	1.91	3.85	4.05	3.8	0.5
Construction	6.38	10.89	15.62	4.5	3.6
Transportation and Storage	1.15	2.04	2.84	4.5	3.3
Communication	1.03	3.12	4.04	6.8	2.6
Utilities	2.40	3.08	2.64	0.5	–1.5
Wholesale Trade	3.97	4.51	5.70	1.8	2.3
Retail Trade	1.71	2.12	2.95	2.7	3.3
Average				2.1	0.9
Manufacturing	2.85	4.46	5.64	3.4	2.3

Source: Statistics Canada, 15-506E and 15-201E.

Note: *Average annual rate of change in percent.

Table 23

Number of Industries in Which Business Services: Wages and Salaries Increased or Decreased Over the Periods 1961-1981 and 1971-1981

	1971–1981 Increase	Decrease	Total
1961–1981			
Increase	21	4	25
Decrease	3	5	8
Total	24	9	33

Source: Table 22.

24. Both ratios show that purchases of business services have risen in relative terms on average and in most industries between 1961 and 1981.

The two ratios differ markedly in their behaviour between 1971 and 1981. RVSB1 increased by 0.9 percent per year (or 43 percent of its 20 year rate of increase) while RVSB2 increased by 6.1 percent per year, which is 145 percent of its 20 year rate of growth. This difference reflects the effect of relatively low operating profits in reducing GDP and raising RVSB2 in 1981.

Analyzing the distribution of the 20 year rates of change in RVSB1 by sector we have the following ranking:

Sector	20-Year Annual Rate of Change in RVSB1
Communications	6.8
Agriculture	4.6
Transportation and Storage	4.5
Construction	4.5
Manufacturing	3.4
Retail Trade	2.7
Wholesale Trade	1.8
Utilities	0.5
Forestry	–1.3
Fishing and Trapping	–1.4

Table 24
Purchases of Business Services: GDP (x 100)
(in 1971 dollars) (RSVB2) by Industry, 1961, 1971 and 1981

	1961	1971	1981	81/61*	81/71*
Agriculture	0.25	0.31	0.69	5.1	8.0
Forestry	0.94	0.81	1.42	2.1	5.6
Fishing and Trapping	0.22	0.27	0.26	0.8	−0.4
Metal Mines	1.89	3.17	12.92	9.6	7.0
Mineral Fuels	7.90	10.37	50.70	9.3	15.9
Non-Metal Mines	2.70	1.79	3.52	1.3	6.8
Mining Services	2.14	1.17	5.23	4.5	15.0
Food and Beverage	3.18	1.86	3.77	0.9	7.1
Tobacco Products	2.29	1.87	2.77	1.0	3.9
Rubber and Plastic	1.97	2.71	3.49	2.9	2.5
Leather	1.50	1.78	2.91	3.3	4.9
Textile	1.54	1.98	10.73	9.7	16.9
Knitting Mills	2.64	1.12	1.37	−3.3	2.0
Clothing Industries	1.06	1.47	1.90	2.9	2.6
Wood	0.93	1.28	1.92	3.6	4.1
Furniture and Fixtures	1.78	1.65	2.26	1.2	3.1
Paper and Allied	1.49	1.54	3.48	4.2	8.2
Printing and Publishing	2.25	2.99	4.44	3.4	4.0
Primary Metals	2.01	1.77	2.73	10.0	4.3
Metal Fabricating	2.21	1.72	2.72	1.0	4.6
Machinery	1.84	2.54	3.76	3.6	3.9
Transportation Equipment	3.53	9.94	16.66	7.8	5.2
Electrical Products	2.41	1.93	3.11	1.3	4.8
Non-Metallic Minerals	1.49	1.36	2.09	1.7	4.3
Petroleum and Coal	1.30	8.21	22.49	14.3	10.1
Chemicals	4.58	3.74	6.18	1.5	5.0
Miscellaneous Manufacturing	1.62	2.67	4.84	5.4	5.9
Construction	4.50	8.37	11.58	4.7	3.2
Transportation and Storage	0.94	1.32	3.53	6.6	9.8
Communication	0.69	1.75	2.19	5.8	2.2
Utilities	0.71	0.87	1.72	4.4	6.8
Wholesale Trade	3.20	3.03	7.40	4.2	8.9
Retail Trade				—	—
Average				4.2	6.1
Manufacturing	2.26	3.03	5.17	4.1	5.3

Source: Statistics Canada, 15-509E and 15-202E.

Note: *Average annual rate of change in percent.

The top and bottom ten industries or sectors in the 20-year annual rate of change in RVSBl are listed along with their respective rates of growth in real output in table 25. The mean rate of growth in output for the ten industries with the greatest increases in RVSB1 is nearly 50 percent greater than the rate of output growth for the bottom ten. Increases in the relative importance of purchased business services tend to be greater in the faster growing industries. We now examine why this might be and whether it has anything to do with contracting out.

Table 25
Industries/Sectors With the Highest and Lowest Rates of Growth in RVSB1 Over the Period 1961-1981

Industry/Sector	Growth in RVSB1	Growth in Real Output
Transportation Equipment	9.0	6.8
Communications	6.8	8.0
Petroleum and Coal Products	5.7	4.0
Agriculture	4.6	2.7
Transportation and Storage	4.5	5.0
Construction	4.5	3.8
Services Incidental to Mining	4.4	8.3
Miscellaneous Manufacturing	3.8	4.3
Metal Mines	3.4	2.2
Textiles	3.3	4.8
Mean		5.0
Fishing and Trapping	–1.4	2.2
Forestry	–1.3	2.3
Primary Metals	–1.2	3.3
Knitting Mills	–0.9	4.8
Food and Beverage	–0.9	3.1
Tobacco Products	–0.5	2.2
Furniture and Fixtures	–0.4	4.4
Non-Metallic Mineral Products	–0.1	3.7
Paper and Allied Products	0	3.5
Metal Fabricating	0.2	4.6
Mean		3.4

Source: Table 24 and Statistics Canada, 15-509E and 15-202E.

An increase in RVSB1 is consistent with an increase in the proportion of service inputs which are supplied externally. It is also consistent, however, with a simple increase in the service intensity of production with no change in contracting out. We demonstrate this as follows:

$$RVSB1 = SE/(SI + OI).$$

SE = Expenditures on external service inputs.

SI = Wage and salary expenditures on internal service inputs.

OI = Wage and salary expenditures on other internal inputs.

If the proportion of service inputs acquired externally increases, then:

$$dSE/SE > dSI/SI.$$

An increase in RVSB1 implies that

$$dSE/SE > a_s\, dSI/SI + (1-a_s)dOI/OI. \quad (1)$$

$$\text{where } a_s = SI/(SI + OI).$$

Subtract dSI/SI from both sides of (1). An increase in RVSB1 also implies the following:

$$dSE/SE - dSI/SI > (a_s-1)dSI/SI + (1-a_s)dOI/OI$$

or

$$dSE/SE - dSI/SI > (1-a_s)(dOI/OI - dSI/SI). \quad (2)$$

The right hand side of (2) is negative for all $dSI/SI > dOI/OI$. Thus, an increase in the internal service intensity of production can cause the ratio RVSB1 to rise, even though the proportion of service inputs acquired externally has remained constant or fallen.

There are several reasons why the service intensity of production may change in both the short-run and the long-run. The demand for nonservice inputs may be more sensitive to the business cycle than the demand for service inputs. This situation is likely if service inputs are associated with overhead (cleaning, security, administration) while nonservice inputs are involved in production activities. Given that the rate of capacity utilization was relatively low in 1981, RVSB1 could have been abnormally high in that year.

The service intensity of production may also increase over the long term for the same reason. If service inputs tend to be used more intensively in overhead activities which have a greater degree of indivisibility than production activities, then the service intensity of industries experiencing secular decline will also increase. Thus, an increase in RVSB1 may be the result of either cyclical excess capacity or secularly declining demand or both.

The service intensity of production may also increase over the long term because of technological change or changes in relative input prices. For example, an increase in the ratio of information systems personnel to production workers may be a consequence of the emergence of computerized inventory management or an increase in the relative cost of holding work-in-process and finished goods inventories. Similarly, an increase in the number of lawyers required to produce a unit of output might be a consequence of increased government regulation or a reinterpretation of tort law (product liability, environmental liability) by the courts.

The service intensity of *domestic* production may also increase if manufacturing activity is shifted offshore since administrators, the intensive users of services, will remain in Canada. In this case, an increase in RVSB1 is reflective of the "hollow corporation" phenomenon where production occurs in the far east while domestic operations are confined to marketing and "paper entrepreneurship." The industries in which the shift to offshore production has been most pronounced include electronics, sporting goods and apparel (Grunwald and Flamm, 1985).

We conclude that while an increase in RVSB1 may reflect contracting-out of business services, it may also be a consequence of an increase in the service intensity of production. Secular changes in demand, technology and the international distribution of production may have contributed to increases in service intensity; the business cycle may also have been a cause. Some of these causes are potentially measurable. Others—such as changes in the production technologies of individual industries—are not readily measurable. Hypothesis testing must take place in a multivariate context, but even this will not be sufficient to remove all ambiguity.

Full scale hypothesis testing is beyond the scope of this study. We confine ourselves to the following observations:

(1) While the business cycle can be adduced to explain the relatively high rate of increase in RVSB2 between 1971 and 1981, the relatively low rate of increase in RVSB1 over the same period is not consistent with a cyclical explanation. Moreover a regression of RVSB2 for the manufacturing sector (with constant, 1971 two-digit weights) on manufacturing capacity utilization and a time trend yields a highly significant positive trend coefficient

along with a significant negative (as expected) coefficient on capacity utilization.

(2) Increases in RVSB1 do not appear to be greater, on average, in industries facing secular decline. Nearly the opposite is true. At least in a bivariate context, it is not true that purchased services have a greater overhead component than wages and salaries in general. The positive association between growth rates of RVSB1 and real output therefore implies one of the following: either the faster growing industries are also experiencing increases in service intensity, or faster growth is associated with contracting-out. The latter supports Stigler's hypothesis that industry growth and vertical specialization are related, but we have already given reasons to doubt this explanation in chapter 2. An alternative explanation for a positive relationship between industry growth and contracting out is that *internally* procured services have a greater fixed or overhead component than purchased services. This proposition will be discussed further in the next section.

(3) Of the industries in which the greatest offshore sourcing is thought to occur, electrical products and clothing report increases in RVSB1 below the average for manufacturing while miscellaneous manufacturing and textiles show above average increases in RVSB1. More systematic measurement of the extent of offshore sourcing is necessary.

(4) The fastest rate of growth in RVSB1 occurs in the transportation equipment industry. This result is consistent with the vertical and horizontal specialization in this industry implied by RVM and RH (see chapter 4). This may be one industry in which contracting-out to the service sector is the most compelling explanation for the observed increase in RVSB1.

VERTICAL SPECIALIZATION OF SERVICE INPUTS: A COMBINED MEASURE

The analysis in the preceding section demonstrates that in most Canadian industries purchases of business services have risen relative to both industry wages and salaries and value added. This does not necessarily imply vertical disintegration with respect to service inputs. This can be inferred only if the rate of growth in business service purchases has exceeded the rate of growth of payments for services performed internally. Thus, a measure of the change in internal expenditures on business services is required.

One solution to this problem was suggested in chapter 4. It involves a comparison of the rate of growth of administrative and other non-manufacturing wages and salaries with the growth rate of residual value added (value added minus rents, quasi-rents and production wages). The key assumptions in this case are that the administrative wage bill is a measure of internal ex-

Table 26

Non-Manufacturing Employee Wages and Salaries: Total Employee Wages and Salaries in Manufacturing (RAT), 1961 and 1981

	1961	1981	Annual Rate of Change
Food and Beverage	45.8	37.1	−1.1
Tobacco Products	31.8	41.1	1.3
Rubber Products*	39.6	32.8	−0.9
Leather Products	26.8	22.0	−1.0
Textiles	33.0	29.7	−0.5
Knitting Mills	27.4	22.7	−0.9
Clothing Industries	29.7	22.0	−1.5
Wood Industries	22.5	20.2	−0.5
Furniture and Fixtures	29.1	23.2	−1.1
Paper and Allied	28.5	28.7	0
Printing and Publishing	46.4	43.8	−0.3
Primary Metals	26.7	30.7	0.7
Metal Fabricating	34.5	29.8	−0.7
Machinery	50.4	38.7	−1.3
Transportation Equipment	35.0	27.9	−1.1
Electrical Equipment	50.5	41.3	−1.0
Non-Metallic Minerals	32.3	31.1	−0.2
Petroleum and Coal	57.0	63.6	0.5
Chemicals	57.1	54.1	−0.3
Miscellaneous Manufacturing	40.5	38.6	−0.2
Manufacturing	38.1	33.9	−0.6

Source: Statistics Canada, 31-203

Note: *Rubber Products is Rubber and Plastic in 1981.

penditures on business services and that the residual component of value added represents purchased services.

An alternative explored in this section is to compare the rate of growth of the administrative wage bill with the growth rate of purchases of business services. If the growth rate of business service purchases exceeds the growth rate of the administrative wage bill, then vertical disintegration has occurred.

The ratio of the administrative wage bill to the total wage bill (RAT) in the manufacturing sector in 1961 and 1981 is reported, along with its rate of change, in table 26. The nonproduction wage bill declined relative to the production wage bill on average and in most industries over this period. This

Table 27
Measures of External and Internal Service Provision: Annual Rates of Change in RVSB1 and RAT and the Implied Rate of Growth in the Ratio of External to Internal Administrative Services, Manufacturing, 1961-1981

	Annual Rate of Change		Difference
	RVSB1	RAT	DDIF
Food and Beverage	–0.9	–1.1	0.2
Tobacco Products	–0.5	1.3	–1.8
Rubber Products	2.2	–0.9	3.1
Leather Products	2.4	–1.0	3.4
Textiles	3.3	–0.5	3.8
Knitting Mills	–0.9	–0.9	0
Clothing Industries	2.5	–1.5	4.0
Wood Industries	2.1	–0.5	2.6
Furniture and Fixtures	–0.4	–1.1	0.7
Paper and Allied	0.1	0	0.1
Printing and Publishing	2.0	–0.3	2.3
Primary Metals	–1.2	0.7	–1.9
Metal Fabricating	0.2	–0.7	0.5
Machinery	2.8	–1.3	4.1
Transportation Equipment	9.1	–1.1	10.2
Electrical Equipment	1.2	–1.0	2.2
Non-Metallic Minerals	–0.1	–0.2	0.1
Petroleum and Coal	5.7	0.5	5.2
Chemicals	1.4	–0.3	1.7
Miscellaneous Manufacturing	3.8	–0.2	4.0
Manufacturing	3.4	–0.6	4.0

Sources: Tables 22 and 26.

result is consistent with a decrease in internal service procurement. There may be other explanations, including a change in production and administrative employees' wage rates and the business cycle. Any cyclical effect would, however, tend to bias the observed rate of change in RAT upwards. Thus, the true long-term decrease in internal administrative services' relative importance is greater than the observed decline in RAT.

The respective annual rates of change in RVSB1 (purchases of business services/wages, salaries and supplementary labour income) and RAT between 1961 and 1981 are reported, along with their difference (DDIF = dRVSB1/RVSB1 - dRAT/RAT) in table 27. Vertical disintegration requires

Table 28
Characteristics of the Industries With the Highest and Lowest Rates of Growth in the Ratio of External to Internal Administrative Services

	DDIF	GDP Growth[1]	Service Use Growth[2]
Top Five			
Transportation Equipment	10.2	6.7	12.3
Petroleum and Coal Products	5.2	1.8	10.8
Machinery	4.1	6.7	10.2
Clothing Industries	4.0	3.0	6.7
Miscellaneous Manufacturing	4.0	4.0	8.8
Mean	5.5	4.4	9.8
Bottom Five			
Primary Metals	–1.9	3.4	9.9
Tobacco Products	–1.8	2.7	8.8
Knitting Mills	0	6.5	6.3
Paper and Allied	0.1	2.6	9.3
Food and Beverage	0.2	3.4	7.6
Mean	–0.7	3.7	8.4

Notes: (1) Annual rate of GDP growth in constant 1971 dollars.
(2) Annual rate of growth of non-production wagebill plus purchases of business services in current dollars.

that this difference be positive—which it is, on average, in 18 of 20 industries. The exceptions are tobacco products and primary metals.

The figures in the third column of table 27 (headed DDIF) can be interpreted as annual rates of change in the ratio of externally to internally procured administrative services. This ratio increased at an annual rate of 10.2 percent in the transportation equipment industry and four percent in the manufacturing.

The results show that administrative services have been contracted out in the manufacturing sector and that the rate at which this has occurred varies from industry to industry. A full analysis of the sources of inter-industry differences in the rate of vertical disintegration is beyond the scope of this study. We confine ourselves to showing that, as table 28 demonstrates, the rate of disintegration has been greater in industries characterized by relatively high rates of growth in both real GDP and total (internal plus external) use of administrative services. The most persuasive explanation for this is that internal administrative services have a larger fixed or overhead component than external services. Even if the marginal effect of an increase in output on the demand for each type of service is the same, the ratio of internal to external services used declines as output increases.[1]

CONCLUSIONS

Using data from the input-output table, we have shown that purchases of business services have increased relative to administrative wages and salaries in most industries over the period 1961-1981. This increase has been greater in faster growing industries. It is consistent with an increase in contracting out of service functions. It could also be a consequence of several other factors.

First, internally produced services may have a greater fixed or overhead component than services acquired externally. Second, the business service category in the input-output table includes data processing equipment rentals. Our results could be due, in part, to an increase in the use of data processing equipment. This problem could be remedied by using the (unpublished) large aggregation of the input-output table which separates services to business management from rentals of data processing equipment. The large aggregation of the input-output table also provides greater detail on other service industries which makes it attractive for future research.

NOTE

1. Let the demand for internal and external services respectively be

$$IS = k_o + k_1 lQ$$

and

$$ES = k_{lQ}$$

Then the ratio of internal to external services is

$$IS/ES = (k_o/k_1 Q) + 1$$

and

$$d(IS/ES)/dQ = - k_0/k_1 Q^2 < 0$$

Chapter 6

LABOUR MARKET ASPECTS OF CONTRACTING OUT

INTRODUCTION

The central focus of this chapter is on contracting out and its relationship to concession bargaining and alterations in work rules. Contracting out and its impact on unions have been the subject of few studies. The exceptions are the automobile industry and those segments of the public sector where privatization has generated controversy. In the automobile industry, out-sourcing has been a major bargaining issue and continues to be an area of concern.

Both concession bargaining and increased contracting out are responses to the changed economic environment of recent years. Both represent a shift from the concern over inflation protection, a dominant bargaining issue in the 1970s, to concern over job security. The primary cause of this change has been the increasing competitive cost pressures on unionized firms in the private sector. These pressures also have been felt in the public sector as a result of actual or proposed privatization measures.

The link between the concession bargaining literature and the contracting out focus of this book is the impact of increased competitive cost pressures on collective bargaining. These pressures explain both wage and work rule concessions and contracting out. In some bargaining situations, it is likely that contracting out can be a substitute for concessions affecting the entire bargaining unit. The circumstances in which a union might prefer allowing some contracting out to reduce the pressure for other concessions are considered in this chapter. We will also consider possible legal barriers to contracting out and collective agreement provisions which limit management's ability to contract out the bargaining unit's work.

PREVIOUS STUDIES

Many studies deal indirectly with contracting out. This review focuses only on studies in which contracting out is the principal issue. The two studies reviewed are those of Young whose work surveyed the Canadian experience primarily during the 1950s[1] and Chandler whose studies focused on the United States.[2]

The study by Young was based on questionnaire returns from both corporations and trade unions in the early 1960s. In his study, Young detected an increase in the extent of contracting out, particularly in the provision of maintenance services in continuous process manufacturing industries. He also noted increases in contracting out by all levels of government, particularly in garbage collection, a trend that continues to the present.

In contrast to the current out-sourcing issue in the automobile industry, Young noted that:

Heavy reliance upon subcontractors was indicated for the performance of work and services in areas peripheral to the main business of the employer. On the other hand, there was little subcontracting of the actual processing and manufacturing of the company's products (Young, p. 5).

The major examples of contracted work in the Young study involved specialized installation and repair rather than routine maintenance that was more likely to be carried out internally. Young also noted the occupational focus of contracted out work. The most frequently contracted out occupations were the various construction crafts and service occupations, particularly trucking, cleaning, cafeteria work and security.

Young's study did not provide a model to explain the decision to contract out a specific activity. His survey responses from employers pointed to a number of reasons for contracting, including the following:

- fluctuating activities with large peak loads
- concern over overtime payments
- costs associated with fringe benefits and administration
- potential labour cost savings and protection against work stoppages.

The employers' responses to Young's questionnaire are probably similar to what many employers responses would be now. The union view of contracting out has changed little. Young found that unions were concerned that employers were trying to avoid paying union wages and negotiating terms and conditions of employment. They were also concerned that increased contracting out would reduce the bargaining power of the remainder of the bargaining unit.

Although there are similarities between contracting out during the time Young studied and now, there are also important differences. In the maintenance and repair contracting examined by Young, much of the work was contracted away from internal union labour to external union labour. The unions losing workers were the industrial unions in manufacturing firms, and the unions gaining members were frequently craft unions representing specialized repair service firms. Now unions are concerned that many firms are contracting out to lower wage non-union labour. The study by Young also dealt with arbitration award restrictions on contracting and prior collective agreement provisions. Both of these issues, in their current context, are discussed below.

A major contribution to the literature on contracting out was made by Margaret Chandler.[3] The core of her results were presented to the 1961 meetings of the Industrial Relations Research Association, but her work generally appears to be less well-known than one would expect given the comprehensive nature of the study and the depth of her insights.

Contracting out of work frequently leads to conflicts between management and unions. Important economic interests are involved and the right to contract is often countered with the union right to retain work. This is particularly true when contracting out involves purchasing components from a foreign supplier, which sometimes happens with current out-sourcing issues. In contrast, Chandler adopted an approach in which the inside and outside labour force are always competing for work offered by the firm. Chandler's specific focus was on industrial maintenance and construction work, so she assumed that much external work would be carried out by members of craft unions. However, her approach can be applied more broadly. Her central argument was the following:

> The heart of the struggle between inside (in-plant) and outside (community craft) forces for industrial maintenance and construction work lies in economic, organizational and technological factors operating behind the scenes and basically shaping the participants' behaviour. These factors overshadow events in the immediate battles between the inside and outside labour forces (Chandler, *IRRA Proceedings*, p. 334).

Chandler proceeded in her analysis on the basis of survey data and interview results. Her approach was wide ranging: she developed a conceptual model of the contracting out process and considered its labour market motivations and results within that framework. For example, she based much of her analysis of the economics of contracting out on Stigler's classic paper on vertical disintegration.[4] Stigler argued that vertical disintegration is likely to be a dominant factor as industries mature. Disintegration allows gains from greater specialization, but this is limited by the extent of the market when industries are in their developing phase. Chandler's focus on organizational issues anticipated at least some of the work of Williamson[5] that was discussed in chapter 2.

From the point of view of this study, the most important aspects of Chandler's work deal with changes in economic circumstances and production technology. Chandler argued that economic upswings usually hasten vertical integration, while downswings and structural changes which increase product market competition hasten vertical disintegration. This is consistent with recent evidence in a wide variety of industries of downsizing in response to both cyclical and structural pressures.

The approach of Chandler has substantial relevance for understanding current contracting out pressures. A number of further points from Chandler's analysis will be developed in later sections of this chapter.

DETERMINANTS AND IMPACTS OF CONTRACTING OUT

In the private sector, contracting out determines the boundary between activities that are internal and external to a given firm. In the public sector, contracting out generally determines the boundary between activities that are conducted by the public sector and activities conducted by the private sector.[6] This section provides a brief review of the costs and benefits of contracting out in both the public and private sector.

Contracting in the Private Sector

The private sector decision to contract out work is somewhat less complex than the corresponding public sector decision. In simplest terms, private firms simply determine the cost of conducting a specific activity internally and externally and then choose the lower cost alternative.

The most obvious costs to examine are production costs for internal and external work. Implicit in the economic analysis of profit-maximizing firms is the assumption that firms are always weighing these relative costs and making adjustments when profitable. In fact, it is not costless to continually review relative costs. There are technical difficulties associated with joint products that increase the complexity of these calculations. It should not be surprising to find management making cost comparisons more frequently when competitive cost pressures increase.

More recently, the emphasis in the economics literature has shifted away from relative production costs internally and externally. A relative production cost advantage for an external supplier is now regarded as necessary but not sufficient to justify the decision to contract out. It is now recognized that the process of contracting itself is not costless: substantial contracting costs can more than offset the production cost advantage of an external supplier. The costs associated with writing and enforcing contracts with external suppliers are referred to as transactions costs.[7]

All market exchanges involve transactions costs. The extent of these costs varies across commodities and exchange relationships. Higher costs of external transactions imply less contracting out. What are the factors influencing transactions costs and, therefore, the extent of contracting out?

Williamson (1979) discussed the characteristics of transactions which have an influence on their costs. His analysis was examined in detail in chapter 2. We concluded in chapter II that contracting out is more costly and thus less likely to occur if:

- it is costly to obtain information about the extent to which the terms of the contract have been met;
- uncertain future events are likely to affect the performance of the contractor;
- irreversible commitments, usually in the form of fixed capital, are necessary in order to carry out the contract.

In many market circumstances, these factors will make it difficult to contract out even if the firm faces higher internal labour costs. The converse of Williamson's conditions is that contracting out is more likely for standardized products produced repetitively with a well-known technology where the contracting parties are not locked into a commitment that is very costly to reverse. In such circumstances, even a relatively modest external labour cost advantage may lead firms to pursue the option of contracting out. The transactions cost framework is useful for analyzing contracting out from an industrial relations perspective because it emphasizes that contracting cost considerations limit the extent to which widespread contracting out is likely to occur.

Contracting in the Public Sector

In principle, the considerations affecting private sector contracting also operate in the public sector. Decision-makers will choose between external and internal provision based on their relative costs. However, the specific elements comprising benefits and costs will differ between the public and private sector. In addition, contracting out in the public sector has been much more publicized in recent years. Governments at all levels have been under increasing pressure to reduce costs with the result that privatization and contracting out have been analyzed in substantial detail.

A number of studies suggest that many public services are more cheaply provided in the private sector.[8] The public choice literature points out, however, that a major cost of this type of contracting out will be a reduction in government control over the process of delivering public services.[9] As in the private sector, the costs of transactions will play a crucial role in determining the extent to which the public sector chooses to contract out different activities.

The potential benefits of contracting out for government are based on reduced costs. These cost savings may be the result of greater economies of scale in the private sector, they may be attributable to product market competition among competing suppliers or they may reflect cost savings based on differences between labour relations systems in the public and private sectors.

On the cost side, the transactions costs considerations discussed above are likely more important in the public sector. Unlike the private sector firm that is assumed to pursue only profit objectives, the public sector organization has both direct objectives (for example, to gain votes by operating an efficient garbage collection service) and distributional and political objectives. Examples of these latter objectives would include job creation, affirmative action and the targeting of benefits to marginal voters. It is likely to be either unfeasible or too costly to pursue distributional and political objectives through contracts with private firms. This limits the range of public sector activities that are likely to be contracted out.[10]

In deciding to use the private sector, labour costs are assessed before any decision to contract out is made. It is frequently considered as a separate category because of the relative importance of labour costs as a fraction of total costs and because of the high visibility of the labour cost question. A number of authors argue that differing labour practices in the private sector contribute to lower costs for work that is contracted out. One U.S. study argues that private sector labour costs are lower because the private sector uses less labour-intensive techniques, offers less liberal vacation and leave benefits, and uses more part-time labour.[11]

Although the factors described above may generate potential cost savings, resistance from public employee unions may increase the political cost of contracting out. The standard union position on contracting out is that the quality of service will fall and that absence of competition among suppliers frequently means that cost savings will not materialize.[12] To the extent that public sector employees constitute a unified block of marginal voters, this may act as a substantial deterrent to contracting out if the efficiency gains are widely dispersed across all voters. Public services are not produced in the least costly way and resources are transferred from taxpayers to members of public sector unions.

EVIDENCE ON CONTRACTING OUT

Most of the existing empirical evidence deals with contracting out from the public sector to the private sector. The extent of contracting out in the private sector is an important issue and is increasingly a bargaining topic, but data are very limited. Much of the evidence on public-private contracting is based on U.S. data, although some evidence for Canada now exists as well. Most of the evidence relates to services provided by municipal governments.

According to Savas,[13] U.S. refuse collection services provided by the private sector generate cost savings of 14 percent relative to municipal provision. The reasons for the lower costs include smaller work crews, less absenteeism, a faster work pace and more efficient vehicles. In his study of 126 Canadian municipalities, McDavid found that after controlling for service levels and city size, public solid waste collection costs were 41 percent above private collection costs.[14]

In a recent study conducted for the Economic Council of Canada, Kitchen[15] examined the relative costs of urban transit services and electric power system maintenance and repair services. He concluded that privately-provided urban transit and contracted out maintenance offered significant cost savings relative to public provision. Although there are differences among the various studies in this area, the general conclusion of most of them is that production of public services through private firms offers the potential for reduced costs.

Summary

This section has reviewed the factors underlying contracting out and some of its impacts in the public sector. The viewpoint of this chapter is that many private and public sector activities are potentially subject to contracting out. This is consistent with Chandler's (1964) view that there is continuing competition between the internal and external labour force for the work of the firm.

The purpose of this general treatment of contracting out is to provide a context for the analysis of the next section. That section considers the collective bargaining aspects of contracting out, specifically the relationship between contracting out, union wages and work rules. However, these factors alone do not explain the contracting decision—it is necessary to hold constant the other factors influencing this decision. In particular, the contracting literature emphasizes that labour and production costs alone do not determine this decision. High monitoring costs (to ensure compliance with the contract), uncertainty and irreversibility all limit the extent to which contracting will occur. These contracting cost considerations are expected to be particularly important in the public sector where distributional and related objectives may increase the overall cost associated with private provision.

CONTRACTING OUT AND CONCESSION BARGAINING

Strategic Aspects of Contracting Out

Concession bargaining is clearly the most important development of this decade in unionized labour markets. It has been the subject of substantial research, but there is not yet complete agreement on its long run impact.[16] The most contentious issue is whether concession bargaining is primarily a reflection of transitory cyclical forces or whether it reflects permanent structural changes. In this chapter we argue that both concession bargaining and increased contracting out reflect structural changes associated with intensified labour market competition from both foreign and domestic non-union suppliers. As a result, they are likely to remain important labour market issues for some time.

Although there are continuing disagreements about the significance of concessions, it is hard to make case that they have not been of substantial importance. It is less clear exactly how contracting out fits into the new industrial relations framework. In some bargaining units, increased contracting out has accompanied wage concessions as firms and unions react to competitive pressures. In other bargaining units, limitations on contracting out have been negotiated as part of a *quid pro quo* for wage concessions. In still other units, it is possible to find increased contracting out of some activities without general wage concessions. In the next section of this chapter, we analyze several different scenarios in a contracting out framework.

In general, concession bargaining occurs only if the alternative to concessions involves layoffs for the bargaining unit's senior members. The voting dynamics of trade unions have frequently been associated with the downward rigidity of union versus non-union wages.[17] The layoff threat must be substantial before it has a significant impact. However, there may be circumstances in which the voting majority of the bargaining unit are able to provide the employer with cost concessions without making concessions related to their own wages.

The best known example of this kind of concession is the two-tier wage system. In agreeing to lower wage rates for new employees, the voting majority of the bargaining unit can increase the competitiveness of the employer without requiring existing members to make sacrifices. In analyzing two-tier wage systems, it is useful to think of the union as a seller of units of labour to the firm. A two-tier wage system is an example of successful price discrimination. There are potential gains to unions from this kind of price discrimination just as there are for firms that are able to discriminate in the product market.

In addition to the gains to existing trade union members from two-tier wage systems relative to broad-based concessions, there are efficiency gains from labour market price discrimination as there is in the product market. The economic inefficiency costs associated with a union wage premium are the result of higher wages restricting employment and output in the union sector.[18] A two-tier wage system reduces the marginal cost of using labour in the union sector and expands employment. If the second tier wage equals the competitive wage, employment in union firms would increase to the competitive level and inefficiency would be minimized. Is it possible to construe at least some contracting out scenarios in this same light?

With a policy of wage standardization, unions will generally contribute to some amount of cross-subsidization within an industrial operation. That is, the relationship between costs and revenues will not be the same for every division or function within a firm and some of this is due to uniform wage policies. Management will have an incentive to contract out those operations that are least profitable subject to the inclusion of contracting costs[19] in this assessment. Other things being equal, activities that are most heavily cross-subsidized should be contracted out first.

Often union leaders will be faced with the requirement of generating a given degree of cost relief for the firm through concessions. Should this be accomplished through across-the-board concessions or through employment reductions in areas where the bargaining unit is least competitive with outside suppliers?[20] The answer to this question will depend on the extent of concessions required, the size of the high cost unit relative to the total bargaining unit and the political resources of the cross-subsidized group. Acceptance by the union of the necessity to contract out high cost operations to preserve wages and jobs for other employees is similar in effect to the wage discrimination associated with two tier wage systems.

In analyzing contracting out as price discrimination, the concept is made clearer by an example. Assume that one theoretical alternative to contracting out would be to reduce the wages of only those union members doing the work that is to be contracted out. Conceptually, at least, this form of price discrimination by the union could provide the same cost relief as contracting out. The internal political dynamics of unions generally prevent this kind of discrimination, but contracting out has similar effects. It allows the union to preserve economic rents for senior members while at the same time providing cost relief to the firm.

THE UNION RESPONSE TO CONTRACTING OUT

Background

Particularly in the public sector, with increased emphasis on privatization, contracting out has become an issue of substantial importance. The Canadian Union of Public Employees (CUPE) argues that most services provided by its members are potentially subject to contracting out. The CUPE response has been to establish a National Task Force on Contracting Out with a mandate to compile information on the extent of contracting out and to coordinate the responses of individual bargaining units.

The negative effects of contracting out on union members, according to CUPE, include the following:

- it reduces employment levels through lay-offs or attrition;
- it increases the scope of the competing non-union sector;
- it reduces the effectiveness of the strike weapon and CUPE bargaining power;
- it leads to pressures to adopt non-union work rules in the bargaining unit;
- it harms the public image of public employees due to the poor quality of contract work.

Although there are some exceptions, current union responses to contracting out have had very limited success. CUPE acknowledges, for example, that employers have the right to contract out unless specifically limited by collective agreement provisions.[21] In the absence of a contracting out clause, unions have tried to use other collective agreement clauses to prevent or slow the pace of contracting out. The specific clauses appealed to and the generally negative results of these attempts are reviewed below.

Unions have tried to challenge management initiatives to contract out work both through the grievance machinery and through direct appeals to labour relations boards. In pursuing the grievance arbitration route, unions have argued that the implied meaning of various contract clauses is to limit contracting out. A clear example of this approach is a grievance based on the recognition clause of the agreement. Such clauses define the scope of the bargaining unit and designate the union as the exclusive bargaining agent. At arbitration, however, the recognition clause has been interpreted as applying to the employees of a firm without implying that the work performed by those employees at the time of certification is legally protected.[22]

If grievance cases are unsuccessful, the other avenue open to unions is the labour relations board. The most frequent grounds for appeal are either successor rights provisions or charges of unfair labour practices. The successor rights provisions have been unsuccessful unless permanent transfers are made involving the entire bargaining unit.

In the case of unfair labour practices, contracting out appears to be a violation of labour relations acts only if it can be demonstrated that the action was undertaken as a result of a specific anti-union policy. For example, if the union can provide evidence that employers acted with the intent of destroying the union, then the unfair labour practice charge likely would be upheld. From the point of view of this study, it appears that it would not be a violation of Canadian labour relations acts to contract out in response to competitive cost pressures.[23] For this reason, the cost pressures facing many firms imply that contracting out may become a more serious problem for organized labour.

The union position, as expressed by CUPE for example, is that legislative changes to limit contracting out are necessary.[24] The proposed legal charges fall in a number of areas including the following:

- mandatory requirement to provide information about contracting out and to bargain;
- application of fair wages clauses based on union rates to contract workers;
- alterations in successor rights legislation to reduce the extent to which work can be contracted out to non-union employees.

The basic intent of the legal changes described above is to take labour out of competition. This has been the intent of supporters of the Wagner Act and its Canadian counterparts since the 1930s. Concession bargaining and other related developments show the long-run failure of this policy.

Labour can be kept out of competition only if there are barriers to entry in product markets. If contracting out by existing union firms is effectively prohibited, this will encourage the growth of entirely non-union competitors.[25] For this reason, legislation of the kind favoured by CUPE and other unions is unlikely to prevent the effects about which unions are concerned. In the short run, however, specific contract language limiting the rights of the employer to contract out may be effective. The extent of provisions of this kind is examined in the following section.

Collective Agreement Provisions

In the current arbitration environment, unions must have a specific and strong collective agreement provision on contracting out if they wish to deter management initiatives in this area. How prevalent are such clauses and what do they imply about current limitations on contracting out?

A number of authors have pointed out the difficulty involved in making inferences about limitations on employers from the existence of contract provisions.[26] The specific wording and its interpretation varies across collective agreements, so that in general it is necessary to know more than whether or not a contract clause exists.[27]

The existence of restrictive collective agreement provisions determines the extent to which contracting out work to the service sector is likely to be important in the future. To assess this issue, we analyze contract provisions in a number of different sectors. We provide data on contracting out provisions in all major Canadian collective agreements with a subsidiary analysis of differences among the largest provinces. We also consider separately the manufacturing sector and that component of the public sector covered by agreements of the Canadian Union of Public Employees.

The data in table 29 and table 30 summarize contract provisions in Canada and the largest provinces for 1980 and 1985. In a time period in which contracting out has been an important bargaining issue, there is no clear trend toward more restrictions either in the national or the Ontario and Quebec data. In British Columbia, fewer employees in 1985 were covered by agreements with no provision and the proportion covered by agreements with some form of restriction increased from 32 percent to 46 percent. B.C.'s change regarding restrictive provisions makes B.C.'s situation similar to Quebec's.

Data on contracting out provisions in the manufacturing sector in 1980 and 1985 are shown in table 31. These data show a small decrease in the fraction of agreements with no contracting out provision and a corresponding increase in contracts with some form of restriction. Comparing the 1985 data in table 31 with the Canadian average data in table 30, we see that manufacturing agreements are more likely to contain restrictive clauses but are also more likely to contain contract language specifically permitting contracting out.

Table 32 presents data on the contracting out provisions found in the collective agreements of the Canadian Union of Public Employees (CUPE) for the nation and for the three largest provinces. CUPE agreements are of particular interest because of the privatization pressures of municipal public services. Nationally, approximately one-third of CUPE members are in

Table 29
Collective Agreement Provisions on Contracting Out, Canada and Selected Provinces, 1980

Contracting Out Provisions	Canada				Ontario				Quebec				British Columbia			
	Agreements		Employees		Agreements		Employees		Agreements		Employees		Agreements		Employees	
	No.	%	No.	%	No.	%	No.	%	No.	%	No.	%	No.	%	No.	%
			(000)				(000)				(000)				(000)	
No provision	562	55.2	1,079	50.6	226	66.0	323	62.3	74	35.0	225	43.9	64	52.0	120	48.9
Complete restriction on work presently performed by bargaining unit	12	1.1	13	0.5	6	1.7	7	1.3	2	0.9	2	0.3	1	0.8	1	0.5
Contracting out restricted if it leads to layoffs	260	25.3	596	27.8	57	16.4	90	17.3	98	46.3	244	47.6	38	30.8	75	30.5
Contracting out permitted	183	17.9	441	20.6	53	15.4	97	18.7	37	17.5	41	8.0	20	16.2	49	19.9
Other	1	0.0	2	0.1	—	—	—	—	—	—	—	—	—	—	—	—

Source: Bureau of Labour Information, Labour Canada.

Table 30

Collective Agreement Provisions on Contracting Out, Canada and Selected Provinces, 1985

Contracting Out Provisions	Canada				Ontario				Quebec				British Columbia			
	Agreements		Employees		Agreements		Employees		Agreements		Employees		Agreements		Employees	
	No.	%	No.	%	No.	%	No.	%	No.	%	No.	%	No.	%	No.	%
			(000)				(000)				(000)				(000)	
No provision	506	52.4	1,007	49.3	200	62.6	281	57.8	55	30.0	222	46.4	61	54.9	81	36.9
Complete restriction on work presently performed by bargaining unit	14	1.4	12	0.5	6	1.8	4	0.8	3	1.6	3	0.5	—	—	—	—
Contracting out restricted if it leads to layoffs	285	29.4	598	29.2	65	20.3	94	19.3	96	52.3	225	46.9	38	34.4	102	46.3
Contracting out permitted	157	16.2	417	20.4	47	14.7	102	20.9	28	15.3	28	5.9	12	10.8	37	16.6
Other	3	0.3	6	0.2	1	0.3	4	0.8	1	0.5	1	0.1	—	—	—	—

Source: Bureau of Labour Information, Labour Canada.

Table 31

Collective Agreement Provisions on Contracting Out, Manufacturing Industries

Contracting Out Provisions	1980				1985			
	Agreements		Employees		Agreements		Employees	
	No.	%	No.	%	No.	%	No.	%
			(000)				(000)	
No Provision	145	46.0	128	29.8	110	40.1	95	26.4
Complete restriction on work presently performed by bargaining unit	5	1.5	4	1.0	10	3.6	7	2.0
Contracting out restricted if it leads to layoffs	90	28.4	144	33.5	90	32.6	129	36.0
Contracting out permitted	75	23.8	151	35.4	63	22.9	126	35.1
Other	—	—	—	—	1	0.3	585	0.1

Source: Bureau of Labour Information, Labour Canada.

Table 32

Collective Agreement Provisions on Contracting Out in Canadian Union of Public Employees' Agreements, Canada and Selected Provinces, 1985

Contracting Out Provisions	Canada				Ontario				Quebec				British Columbia			
	Agreements		Employees		Agreements		Employees		Agreements		Employees		Agreements		Employees	
	No.	%	No.	%	No.	%	No.	%	No.	%	No.	%	No.	%	No.	%
			(000)				(000)				(000)				(000)	
No provision	910	39	81,882	33	470	44	45,798	39	15	7	233	1	125	35	8,974	34
Complete restriction on work presently performed by bargaining unit	150	7	10,819	4	39	4	1,197	1	9	4	6,203	22	15	4	992	4
No contracting if bargaining unit can perform work	19	1	2,850	1	2	0.2	62	0.1	—	—	—	—	8	2	1,847	7
Employer may contract but must guarantee jobs of all existing employees	925	40	95,297	39	399	37	43,804	38	170	75	17,115	60	175	49	9,896	38
Job guarantees for workers with specified seniority	150	7	24,496	10	101	9.5	17,664	15	26	11	4,768	17	4	1	76	0.3
Employer will consult with or notify union or will endeavour to find work for displaced employees	141	6	29,408	12	47	5	5,993	5	5	2	5	0.1	17	5	3,529	14
Other	24	1	3,021	1	8	1	1,685	2	3	1	349	1	10	3	819	3

Source: Canadian Union of Public Employees, System for the Analysis of Labour Agreement Data.

bargaining units with no contracting out protection in their agreement. Very few agreements provide for a complete restriction on contracting out. However, nearly 50 percent of agreements protect either all current employees in the bargaining unit or those with a specified level of seniority. Although the coding schemes for the agreements differ slightly, a comparison of tables 30 and 32 suggests that CUPE agreements have more restrictive provisions than agreements in other sectors.

Differences among the largest provinces are also shown in table 32. Ontario and British Columbia do not deviate significantly from the national average data for CUPE agreements discussed above. Quebec, however, differs in a number of respects from the national average. These differences are clearest in the first two rows and the fourth row of table 32. Contrary to the average experience, very few Quebec CUPE members are in bargaining units whose agreements provide no protection against contracting out. In fact, 22 percent of Quebec CUPE members have contracts completely limiting contracting out. Protection for all existing bargaining unit members is provided in contracts covering 60 percent of CUPE members in Quebec while a further 17 percent of employees have clauses providing similar protection for senior workers.

A complete explanation for the situation in Quebec with respect to contracting out provisions is beyond the scope of this study. A number of authors have analyzed the bargaining power of Quebec public sector unions and concluded that their strength exceeds that of public sector unions in the rest of Canada.[28] It is also the case that restrictions on contracting out in the public sector may be more effective than in the private sector due to the barriers to entry associated with the presence of natural monopoly in providing local public services.

CONCLUSIONS

Any changes that increase the extent of competition faced by unionized firms increase the pressure for and extent of contracting out. Freer trade, deregulation and reduced entry barriers all act to encourage contracting out.[29] Particularly in the private sector, these pressures will be difficult for unions to resist. To the extent that contract clauses do limit the amount of work that is contracted out, this will increase the pressure for concessions affecting the entire bargaining unit. There are, however, limits to this process. Contracting out is not a panacea for all of the cost problems of firms. Some activities do not lend themselves well to contracting out. This is particularly the case if contracted outputs are difficult and costly to monitor, if their production is subject to the effects of uncertainty or if irreversible capital investments are required. In spite of such limitations on the feasibility of contracting, it is likely to become an increasingly important management approach to cost containment. This implies continuing growth in the contracting out of services.

The most effective union response is to develop effective collective agreement language to limit contracting out. In the public sector, such clauses are likely to be more effective and easier to negotiate than in the private sector where competitive forces to minimize costs operate more directly. It may be in the interest of at least some unions to allow contracting out in order to make the employer more competitive and preserve union wages for high seniority workers in other jobs. This consideration provides the link between contracting out and concession bargaining.

In future work in this area, we hope to integrate the approach of this chapter with the empirical work on contracting out in chapter 3. In particular, we intend to explore the determinants of contracting out in more detail and to assess the extent to which union wage premiums play an important role in this process.

NOTES

1. F.J.L. Young, *The Contracting Out of Work* (Industrial Relations Centre, Queen's University, 1964).
2. Margaret K. Chandler, *Management Rights and Union Interests*, (McGraw-Hill, 1964) and "Competition Between the Inside and Outside Labour Force for the Work of the Industrial Firm," *IRRA Proceedings*, 1961, pp. 334-345.
3. The initial monograph from which the later Chandler work developed is: Margaret K. Chandler and Leonard R. Sayles, *Contracting Out: A Study of Management Decision-Making*, Graduate School of Business Administration, Columbia University, New York, 1959.
4. George Stigler, "The Division of Labor is Limited by the Extent of the Market," *Journal of Political Economy* 1951, pp. 185-193.
5. Oliver Williamson, "Transactions Cost Economics: The Governance of Contractual Relations," *Journal of Law and Economics*, V. XXII (1979), pp. 233-261.
6. Some contracting out may be from one public sector or organization to another leaving the public-private boundary unaffected.
7. Much of this literature is associated with Williamson (1979). This literature is reviewed and applied to the contracting out of services in R. Dobell, J. McRae and M. Desbois, *The Service Sector in the Canadian Economy* (Ottawa, Institute for Research on Public Policy, 1984), pp. 24-32.
8. See, for example, E.S. Savas, *The Organization and Efficiency of Solid Waste Collection* (Lexington, Mass: Lexington Books, 1977).
9. These issues are also considered in M.W. Reder, "The Theory of Employment and Wages in the Public Sector" in D. Hamermesh (ed.), *Labor in the Public and Nonprofit Sectors* (Princeton University Press, 1975).
10. A number of authors regard this as a benefit of privatization. If political or redistribution objectives become more costly to pursue, their quantity will decline. See D.G. McFetridge, "The Efficiency Consequences of Privatization" in W.T. Stanbury and T.E. Kierans (eds.), *Papers on Privatization* (Ottawa, Institute for Research on Public Policy, 1985), pp. 109-129.
11. Barbara J. Stevens (ed.), *Delivering Municipal Services More Efficiently: A Comparison of Municipal and Private Service Delivery* (Washington, U.S. Department of Housing and Urban Development, 1984).

12. The union view of contracting out is considered in more detail below.
13. E.S. Savas, "Competitive Costs of Public and Private Enterprise in a Municipal Service" in W.J. Baumol (ed.), *Public and Private Enterprise in a Mixed Economy* (St. Martin's Press, New York, 1980), pp. 253-263.
14. J. McDavid, "The Canadian Experience with Privatizing Residential Solid Waste Collection Services," *Public Administration Review*, September, 1985, pp. 602-608.
15. H. Kitchen, *Local Government Enterprise in Canada* (Ottawa, Economic Council of Canada, 1986).
16. For a general review of concession bargaining and its causes, see Kochan, Katz and McKersie (1986).
17. Union voting models are discussed in W.N. Atherton, *Theory of Union Bargaining Goals* (Princeton University Press, 1973).
18. The classic partial equilibrium analysis of this effect is Albert Rees, "The Effects of Unions on Resource Allocation," *Journal of Law and Economics*, October, 1963, pp. 69-78.
19. Outputs that are separable from the production process where monitoring costs are low and uncertainty limited are most likely to be contracted out on these grounds.
20. During the 1979-80 time period when the future of the firm was in doubt, Chrysler Corporation costed all operations where work potentially could be contracted out. It threatened to close specific facilities if the bargaining unit could not adjust some combination of wages or work rules to make internal production competitive with external supply.
21. CUPE Education Department, *The Legal Impact of Contracting-Out and Privatization on the Collective Bargaining Relationship*, mimeo for the National Conference on Contracting Out, 1987.
22. The precedent setting arbitration case on contracting out is *Russel Steel vs. United Steelworkers* (1966). The arbitrator, Harry Arthurs, ruled that contracting out was permissible unless specifically prohibited by the contract. Arthurs' view was that the right to contract out was well known to unions and therefore the absence of a contracting out clause implied the inability of the union to negotiate it. For an opposing view, see B. Langille, "Equal Partnership in Canadian Labour Law," *Osgoode Hall Law Journal* (1983), pp. 532-536.
23. The timing of contracting out may affect its legal status in terms of the requirement to bargain in good faith. Like technological change prior

to the legislative developments triggered by the Freedman Report, contracting out can be timed opportunistically to coincide with the beginning of the closed period of the collective agreement. Proponents of the union point of view argue that bargaining should be mandatory over contracting out.

24. CUPE may not be entirely representative since the threat of privatization directly affects nearly all of its bargaining units.

25. Natural monopoly elements of many local public services may make the achievement of this objective easier for CUPE than for private sector unions.

26. See, for example, Chandler (1964), p. 217.

27. There have been relatively few studies examining contract provisions. For an early study, see L.E. Lunden, "Subcontracting Clauses in Major Contracts," *Monthly Labour Review*, June 1961, pp. 581-586 and July 1961, pp. 715-723.

28. Note that the CUPE agreements referred to here cover only a subset of all public employees in Quebec. For one analysis of Quebec public sector bargaining, see Gerard Hebert, "Public Sector Bargaining in Quebec: A Case of Hypercentralization" in Mark Thompson and Gene Swimmer (eds.), *Conflict or Compromise: The Future of Public Sector Industrial Relations* (Ottawa, IRPP, 1984), pp. 229-282.

29. Chandler (1964) argued that management was likely to continue to be in the dominant position on this issue. Her conclusion was: "In general, management seemed to gain by default its 'right' to contract out. Flexibility, sufficient to adapt to current need, was provided, not by grace of foresighted planning or insightful dispute settlement, but rather by virtue of the difficulty of any one group's mapping out and effectuating a strong program of control. The diverse and competing groups were limited to competition within the range of the few, and not always significant, variables they were able to control," Chandler (1964), p. 308.

Chapter 7

Conclusions

SCOPE OF THIS STUDY

Our general objective in this study has been to investigate the causes of vertical specialization and to assess their impact on the service sector of the Canadian economy. Our specific objectives were to determine the following:

- the functions which have tended to be contracted out
- the industries which have tended to contract out
- the consequences of contracting out for the industrial distribution of employment.

While our study contains a great deal of information relevant to these issues, it falls short of achieving these specific objectives. This is in part a consequence of the preliminary nature of this study. We make a number of suggestions regarding the type of future research necessary.

The limited nature of our results is also due to the fact that, to the best of our knowledge, there have been no previous attempts to derive a measure of vertical specialization in service functions which can be calculated for a large number of industries using published data. The value added to shipments ratio is a widely used measure of vertical integration in manufacturing. Although we calculated this ratio and analyze its behaviour, we also noted that it tells us nothing about vertical specialization in intermediate services.

MEASURING VERTICAL SPECIALIZATION

The bulk of our empirical effort has been devoted to deriving and examining the behavior of alternative measures of vertical specialization. Each of our measures is limited in coverage and each requires that assumptions be made about the underlying demand for services. Together, however, they provide an interesting and useful picture.

While we engaged only in the crudest hypothesis testing, we have developed a framework for more extensive testing. The discussion of the transactions cost hypothesis in chapter 2 provides some guidance and some warnings. Other things being equal, contracting out will occur if it becomes less hazardous to deal with independent suppliers. The important question is what reduces the hazards (contracting costs) of dealing with arm's-length suppliers. The general answer is that contracting costs are reduced as the product involved becomes standardized, that is, as its technical characteristics become well known and the number of potential users and sellers increases. This may but need not be associated with growing demand.

The implication is that the most effective tests of the transactions cost hypothesis will be conducted at the product rather than the industry level. Considerable insight regarding the relationship between specialization, complexity and the cost of arm's-length contracting can be found in the studies of railway freight cars, automobile parts, aerospace components and electronic goods summarized in chapter 2.

Tests of the transactions cost hypothesis at the industry level are problematic. While products and processes can be mature and this can be measured, the same is not true of the industry categories for which data are published. Are the clothing and textile industries more mature than they were fifteen years ago? Many would argue the contrary. Are the clothing and textile industries more mature than the chemical industry? A case could be made in either direction.

Thus, although the simple cross-sectional comparison we undertook in chapter 5 implies that the contracting out of business services increased faster in the faster growing industries, we are not inclined to infer causality—let alone a maturity or an economies of scale explanation. Tests of hypotheses regarding the impact of unionization on contracting out at the aggregate industry level are more appealing. Even here, considerable care must be taken in that the incentive to contract out and the ability of workers to stop it are both increasing functions of the degree of unionization, particularly in the short run.

We would not expect the contracting out of business services in general or of accounting services in particular to depend on unionization since the employees involved would not normally be members of the bargaining unit. Unionization is potentially a factor in the case of janitors and security guards. The simple cross-tabulations presented in chapter 3 provide little evidence of an important union impact. For security guards, there is considerable contracting out by all industries, but only a slight indication that this is in response to greater unionization. In the case of janitors, there is widespread contracting in occurring in the manufacturing industries and, in fact, there is a weak positive relationship between more contracting in and higher unionization ratios.

A defect of our measurement of the effect of unions is that it is based on industry rather than firm data. If unionized firms in a particular industry are contracting out while non-union firms are contracting in, we could draw incorrect conclusions about the union effect from industry data.

The measures of vertical specialization derived and analyzed in this study can be applied more broadly. Changes in the industrial distribution of employment can be calculated for a wider range of occupational groups using the decennial census. Changes in the consumption of so-called "personal" services (including machinery rentals and services to buildings and dwellings) by industry can be calculated from the input-output table. Refinement of contracting-out measures is possible for those with access to the large aggregation of the input-output table. For some narrow classes of services (services to buildings and dwellings) an unambiguous measure of contracting out could be obtained by combining data from the large aggregation of the input-output table and the decennial census respectively.

Alternative sources of data also require further exploration. Our analysis of vertical specialization in legal services in chapter 3 illustrates the benefits of collecting data on more precisely defined occupations. The accuracy of our estimated rate of contracting out of legal services in manufacturing depends on the validity of the assumption that the growth in the lawyer intensity of manufacturing is the same as the growth in the lawyer intensity of the economy. This, in turn, requires us to assume that the relative importance of corporate law remained constant over the observation period. It probably did not. Our analysis of the distribution of membership in the Patent and Trademark Institute of Canada is not burdened by this problem. It indicates some tendency to contract out patent and trademark work over the last thirty years. Conversations with PTIC officials indicate that one reason for this is increasing specialization within the discipline (that is, licenses, litigation, et cetera). A firm would require a much larger patent or trademark portfolio to occupy a set of specialists than was formerly needed to occupy a general intellectual property lawyer.

UNIONS AND CONTRACTING OUT

In chapter 6, we analyzed the relationship between unionization and contracting out in both the private sector and the public sector. We argued that a transactions costs framework is necessary to assess the extent to which firms will contract out in response to high costs of internal production in a union context.

We related contracting out to the broader range of possible responses of unionized firms to competitive cost pressures. In recent years, many collective bargaining concessions have been made by unions, so we provided an analysis of how contracting out is likely to relate to other concessions. We concluded that a collective agreement that allows more contracting out by the employer may act as a substitute for other contract concessions. In this way, it can act as a form of price discrimination through which unions can preserve economic rents for senior members while at the same time providing cost relief to the firm.

Our analysis of unions and contracting out is applicable to situations in which unionized firms face competitive cost pressures and require a given degree of cost relief. In what circumstances will the union choose to allow more contracting out in preference to a policy of uniform wage reductions for all members of the bargaining unit?

We have shown that wage standardization policies of unions create differing ratios of individual wage rates to their opportunity cost. This is equivalent to cross-subsidization within the bargaining unit. If transactions costs are held constant, activities that are most heavily subsidized should be contracted out first. In this context, contracting out is more likely if the extent of concessions required is small, if the high-cost group is small relative to the total bargaining unit and if the high cost group does not contain high seniority members with the ability to prevent such concessions.

We have also provided some evidence on contractual barriers to contracting out in major Canadian collective agreements. We included an analysis of collective agreement provisions in the manufacturing sector and in the agreements of the Canadian Union of Public Employees. We found no clear trend toward limitations on contracting out. We noted the existence of more restrictive contract clauses in Quebec than in other jurisdictions, but we conclude that existing collective agreement provisions should not act as a substantial barrier to contracting out in response to competitive cost pressures facing unionized employers.

SUMMARY MEASURES OF CONTRACTING OUT

How important is contracting out in explaining the growth of the service sector? The results of this study are exploratory in nature but two of the methods that we develop do provide useful measures of this phenomenon and are discussed in the following paragraphs.

Our first set of measures is derived from the decennial census which provides data on employment by sector, industry and occupation for the years 1961, 1971 and 1981. Our preferred approach is to infer that contracting out has occurred in a given sector and occupation if the proportion of sectoral employment accounted for by that occupation has decreased more (increased less) than the proportion of total (economy-wide) employment accounted for by the same occupation.

In Chapter 3, we applied our method to four occupations. These are: accountants, security guards, janitors and lawyers. We chose these occupations because each has a readily identifiable "home industry" to which jobs contracted out by other sectors would naturally flow. For example, janitorial jobs contracted out by the manufacturing sector should show up in the industry "Services to Buildings and Dwellings." We can then calculate the proportion of the observed growth of this industry which is due to contracting out.

Of course, contracting out estimates can be obtained for any service or other occupational class (chauffeurs, programmers, etc.) whether they have a readily identifiable "home industry" or not. This task is left for the future.

Our estimates of the number of jobs contracted out by the manufacturing sector over the periods 1961-71 and 1971-81 together with the respective proportions of "home industry" employment growth they account for are reported in table 33. Our estimates of contracting out by all sectors other than services and public administration appear in table 34. In only one case, security guards, is there an unambiguous indication of sustained and significant contracting out. In the other cases, depending on the level of aggregation and the time period either contracting out or contracting in can be inferred. Taking these four occupations together, contracting out by all the industrial sectors of the economy (i.e., all sectors other than services and public administration) accounts for none of the growth of the relevant home industries over the 1961-71 period and 26.6 percent of the growth over the 1971-81 period.

The employment implications of our input-output based measure of contracting out can be estimated, albeit roughly. One approach is to assume that the value of intermediate services produced internally by the manufacturing sector is given by non-production wages and salaries (from the Census of Manufactures) and that the value of externally produced intermediate services is given by purchases of business services as reported in the input-output table. We can then estimate that manufacturing employment would have been in 1981 if the ratio of purchases of business services to non-production wages and salaries had remained at its 1961 value.

The details of this calculation are reported in table 35. Manufacturing employment would have been higher by about 54 thousand or 2.9 percent in 1981 if the ratio of purchased business services to non-production wages and salaries had remained at its 1961 value. This "transfer" of 54 thousand jobs

Table 33

Census Based Estimates of Contracting Out by the Manufacturing Sector

Occupation	Number of Employees		Percent Home Industry Employment Growth Accounted for	
	1961–71	1971–81	1961–71	1971–81
Accountants	2240	638	27.0	5.0
Security Guards	4495	2400	60.6	16.0
Janitors	–5290	–419	—	—
Lawyers	–18	19	—	0.1

Source: See tables 3, 6, 9, 12.

Table 34

Census-based Estimates of Contracting Out by All Sectors Other than Services and Public Administration

Occupation	Number of Employees		Percent Home Industry Employment Growth Accounted for	
	1961–71	1971–81	1961–71	1971–81
Accountants	–10114	7750	—	60.6
Security Guards	5894	5380	79.4	35.8
Janitors	–1437	3309	—	16.6
Lawyers	–80	117	—	0.8
Total	–5737	16556	—	26.6

Sources: See tables 3, 6, 9, 12.

would "explain" some 14 percent of the growth in employment in the Business Services sector over the period 1961-81.

It is difficult to compare the employment shift estimates obtained with input-output data with the earlier estimates derived from the decennial census. The input-output category "purchases of business services" covers a broad range of service inputs (including advertising and data processing rentals) but excludes janitorial services. The two approaches do reach similar conclusions. Contracting out service functions has had a small negative effect on observed manufacturing employment and a larger, positive effect on observed service sector employment.

Table 35
The Effect of Contracting Out on Manufacturing Employment: An Estimate Based on Input-Output and Census of Manufactures Data

	Year	
	1961	1981
(1) Non-production wages and salaries in manufacturing	$2,169 million	$12,563 million
(2) Purchases of business services by the manufacturing sector	171	2,411
(3) (1) + (2)	2,340	14,974
(4) (1) / (3)	.927	.839
(5) Non-production employment in manufacturing	413,192	516,397
(6) Estimated non-production wages and salaries with no increase in contracting out over 1961: .927 x 14,974 = $13,880 million		
(7) Additional non-production wages and salaries if no increase in contracting out over 1961: $13,880 – 12,563 = $1,318 million		
(8) Wages and salaries per non production worker, 1981: $12,563 / 516.4 = $24,328		
(9) Additional manufacturing employment with no increase in contracting out: 1,318,000 / 24,328 = 54,134		

Sources: Statistics Canada 31-203, 15-506E and 15-201E.

Our overall assessment is that the contracting out of services is an important phenomenon. Our results show that there is sufficient evidence of this to warrant refinements and extension of these results. The census-based measures show that more than a quarter of the increase in service sector employment is accounted for by contracting out of the four occupations analyzed between 1971 and 1981. These findings indicate that a more detailed understanding of contracting out is necessary if we are to interpret the growth of the Canadian service sector correctly.

References

Anderson, E. and Schmittlein, D., "Integration of the Sales Force: An Empirical Examination," *Rand Journal of Economics*, 15, Autumn 1984, pp. 385-95.

Atherton, W.N., *Theory of Union Bargaining Goals*, Princeton: Princeton University Press, 1973.

Buzzell, R., "Is Vertical Integration Profitable?," *Harvard Business Review*, 61, 1983, pp. 92-102.

Canadian Union of Public Employees, "The Legal Impact of Contracting-Out and Privatization on the Collective Bargaining Relationship," mimeo, 1987.

Carr, J. and Mathewson, F., "The Economics of the Organization of Legal Firms" (Mimeo, Department of Economics, University of Toronto), 1987.

Casson, M., *The Firm and the Market*, Cambridge: MIT Press, 1987.

Casson, M., "Multinational Firms," in R. Clarke and T. McGuinness (eds.), *The Economics of the Firm*, Oxford: Basil Blackwell, 1987.

Caves, R., *Multinational Enterprise and Economic Analysis*, Cambridge: Cambridge University Press, 1982.

Chandler, Margaret K. and Sayles, Leonard R., *Contracting-Out: A Study of Management Decision-Making*, New York: Graduate School of Business Administration, Columbia University, 1959.

Chandler, Margaret K., "Competition Between the Inside and Outside Labor Force for the Work of the Industrial Firm," *Proceedings of the Industrial Relations Research Association*, 1961, pp. 334-335.

Chandler, Margaret K., *Management Rights and Union Interests*, New York: McGraw-Hill, 1964.

Cheung, S., "The Contractual Nature of the Firm," *Journal of Law and Economics*, 26, April 1983, pp. 1-21.

Coase, R., "The Nature of the Firm," *Economica*, 4, 1937, pp. 386-405.

Davies, S., "Vertical Integration," in R. Clarke and T. McGuinness (eds.), *The Economics of the Firm*, Oxford: Basil Blackwell, 1987.

Davidson, W.H. and D.G. McFetridge, "International Technology Transactions and the Theory of the Firm," *The Journal of Industrial Economics*, 32, March, 1984, pp. 253-65.

____, “Key Characteristics in the Choice of International Technology Transfer Mode,” *Journal of International Business Studies*, 16, Summer, 1985, pp. 5-22.

Dobell, R., McRae, J., and Desbois, M., *The Service Sector in the Canadian Economy*, Ottawa: IRPP, 1984.

Eccles, R., “The Quasifirm in the Construction Industry,” *Journal of Economic Behaviour and Organization*, Vol. 2, December 1981, pp. 335-58.

Eckstein, O., and Wilson, T.A., “The Determination of Money Wages in American Industry,” *Quarterly Journal of Economics*, August 1962, pp. 379-414.

Ethier, W., “The Multinational Firm,” *Quarterly Journal of Economics*, 101, November 1986, pp. 805-34.

Globerman, S., and Schwindt, R., “The Organization of Vertical Related Transactions in the Canadian Forest Products Industries,” *Journal of Economic Behavior and Organization*, Vol. 7, June 1986, pp. 199-212.

Grossman, S. and Hart, O., “The Costs and Benefits of Ownership: A Theory of Lateral and Vertical Integration,” *Journal of Political Economy*, 94, August 1986, pp. 691-719.

Grunwald, J. and K. Flamm, *The Global Factory*, Washington: The Brookings Institution, 1985.

Harrigan, K., “A Framework for Looking at Vertical Integration,” *Journal of Business Strategy*, 3, 1983, pp. 30-37.

Hebert, Gerard, “Public Sector Bargaining in Quebec: A Case of Hypercentralization,” in M. Thompson and E. Swimmer (eds.), *Conflict or Compromise: The Future of Public Sector Industrial Relations*, Ottawa: IRPP, 1984, pp. 229-282.

Horstman, I. and Markusen, J., “A Formal Model of the Multinational Enterprise: New Theoretical Tools for Old Stylized Facts,” Paper presented at the Annual Meetings of the American Economics Association, New Orleans, December 1986.

Horstman, I. and Markusen, J., “Licensing versus Direct Investment: A Model of Internalization by the Multinational Enterprise,” *Canadian Journal of Economics*, 20, August 1987, pp. 464-8.

Joskow, P., “Contract Duration and Relationship-Specific Investments: Evidence from Coal Markets,” *American Economic Review*, 77, March 1987, pp. 168-87.

Katz, H.C., *Shifting Gears: Changing Labor Relations in the U.S. Automobile Industry*, Cambridge: M.I.T. Press, 1985.

Kitchen, H., *Local Government Enterprise*, Ottawa: Economic Council of Canada, 1986.

Klein, B., Crawford, R., and Alchian, A., "Vertical Integration, Appropriable Rents and the Competitive Contracting Process," *Journal of Law and Economics*, 21, October 1978, pp. 297-326.

Kochan, T.A., Katz, H.C., and McKersie, R.B., *The Transformation of American Industrial Relations*, New York: Basic Books, 1986.

Langille, B., "Equal Partnership in Canadian Labour Law," *Osgoode Hall Law Journal*, 1983, pp. 532-536.

Levy, D., "Testing Stigler's Interpretation of Division of Labor is Limited by the Extent of the Market," *Journal of Industrial Economics*, 32, March 1984, pp. 377-90.

Levy, D., "The Transactions Cost Approach to Vertical Integration: An Empirical Examination," *Review of Economics and Statistics*, 67, 1985, pp. 438-45.

Lunden, L.E., "Subcontracting Clauses in Major Contracts," *Monthly Labour Review*, June 1961, pp. 581-586 and July 1961, pp. 715-723.

Mariotti, S., and Cainarca, G.C., "The Evolution of Transaction Governance in the Textile-Clothing Industry," *Journal of Economic Behavior and Organization*, Vol. 7, December 1986, pp. 351-374.

Masten, S., "The Organization of Production: Evidence from the Aerospace Industry," *Journal of Law and Economics*, 27, October 1984, pp. 403-17.

Mathewson, F., and Winter, R., *Competition Policy and Vertical Exchange*, Toronto: University of Toronto Press, 1985.

McCracken, B.H., "Why Are Business and Professional Services Growing So Rapidly?," Federal Reserve Bank of Atlanta, *Economic Review*, 70, August, 1985, pp. 14-28.

McDavid, J., "The Canadian Experience with Privatizing Residential Solid Waste Collection Services," *Public Administration Review*, September 1985, pp. 602-608.

McFetridge, D.G., "The Efficiency Consequences of Privatization," in W.T. Stanbury and T.E. Kierans (eds.), *Papers on Privatization*, Ottawa: IRPP, 1985.

McFetridge, D.G., "The Timing, Mode and Terms of Technology Transfer: Some Recent Findings," in A.E. Safarian and G.Y. Bertin, eds.,

Multinationals, Governments and International Technology Transfer, London, Croom Helm, 1986.

McKean, R., "Discussion," *American Economic Review*, 61, May 1971, pp. 124-5.

McManus, J., "The Costs of Alternative Economic Organizaitons," *Canadian Journal of Economics*, 8, August 1975, pp. 334-50.

Meltz, N.M., "Labour Movements in Canada and the United States," in T. Kochan (ed.), *Challenges and Choices Facing American Labor*, Cambridge: M.I.T. Press, 1985, pp. 5-334.

Monteverde, K. and Teece, D., "Supplier Switching Costs and Vertical Integration in the Automobile Industry", *Bell Journal of Economics*, 13, Spring 1982, pp. 206-13.

Palay, T., "Comparative Institutional Economics: The Governance of Rail Freight Contracting," *The Journal of Legal Studies*, Vol. 13, June 1984, pp. 265-88.

Perry, M., "Vertical Integration: Determinants and Effects," Morristown, N.J.: Bell Communications Research, mimeo, 1987.

Reder, M.W., "The Theory of Employment and Wages in the Public Sector," in D. Hamermesh (ed.), *Labor in the Public and Nonprofit Sectors*, Princeton: Princeton University Press, 1975.

Rees, Albert, "The Effects of Unions on Resource Allocation," *Journal of Law and Economics*, October, 1963, pp. 69-78.

Savas, E.S.,*The Organization and Efficiency of Solid Waste Collection*, Lexington: Lexington Books 1977.

Savas, E.S., "Comparative Costs of Public and Private Enterprise in a Municipal Service," in W.J. Baumol (ed.), *Public and Private Enterprise in a Mixed Economy*, New York: St. Martin's Press, 1980, pp. 253-264.

Silver, M., *Enterprise and the Scope of the Firm*, Oxford: Martin Robertson, 1984.

Statistics Canada, *The Input-Output Structure of the Canadian Economy 1961-71*, Catalogue 15-506E, Ottawa, 1977.

Statistics Canada, *The Input-Output Structure of the Canadian Economy in Constant Prices, 1961-74*, Catalogue 15-509E, Ottawa, 1979.

Statistics Canada, *The Input-Output Structure of the Canadian Economy, 1979-81*, Catalogue 15-201E, Ottawa, 1985.

Statistics Canada, *The Input-Output Structure of the Canadian Economy in Constant Prices, 1979-81*, Catalogue 15-202E, Ottawa, 1985.

Statistics Canada, *Manufacturing Industries of Canada: National and Provincial Areas,* Catalogue 31-203, Ottawa, Annual.

Statistics Canada, *Industrial Corporations: Financial Statistics,* Catalogue 61-003, Ottawa, Quarterly.

Stevens, B.J. (ed.), *Delivering Municipal Services More Efficiently,* Washington: U.S. Department of Housing and Urban Development, 1984.

Stigler, G., "The Divsion of Labour Is Limited by the Extent of the Market," *Journal of Political Economy,* 59, June 1951, pp. 185-93.

Teece, D., "Towards an Economic Theory of the Multiproduct Firm," *Journal of Economic Behavior and Organization,* Vol. 3, March 1982, pp. 39-64.

Teece, D., "Transactions Cost Economics and the Multinational Enterprise: An Assessment," *Journal of Economic Behavior and Organization,* Vol. 7, March 1986, pp. 21-46.

Tucker, I. and Wilder, R., "Trends in Vertical Integration in the U.S. Manufacturing Sector," *Journal of Industrial Economics,* 26, September 1977, pp. 81-94.

Waterson, M., *Economic Theory of the Industry,* Cambridge: Cambridge University Press, 1984.

Williamson, O., *Markets and Hierarchies: Analysis and Antitrust Implications,* New York: The Free Press, 1975.

Williamson, O., "Transactions Cost Economics: The Governance of Contractual Relations," *Journal of Law and Economics,* Vol. XXII, 1979, pp. 233-261.

Williamson, O., "Vertical Integration and Related Variations on a Transaction-Cost Economics Theme," in J. Stiglitz and F. Mathewson (eds.), *New Developments in the Analysis of Market Structure,* Cambridge: MIT Press, pp. 149-75.

Williamson, O.E., M. Wachter and J. Harris, "Understanding the Employment Relation: The Analysis of Idiosyncratic Exchange," *Bell Journal of Economics,* Spring, 1975, pp. 250-80.

Worthy J., *Shaping an American Institution: Robert E. Wood and Sears Rosebuck,* Urbana: University of Illinois Press, 1984.

Young, F.J.L., *The Contracting Out of Work,* Industrial Relations Centre, Queen's University, 1964.

